Tideways & Byways
in
Essex & Suffolk

Tideways & Byways in Essex & Suffolk

By

ARCHIE WHITE

Illustrated by the Author

IAN HENRY PUBLICATIONS
1979

First published by
Edward Arnold & Co., Ltd.

This edition, 1977
Reprinted 1979

ISBN 0 86025 814 9

Made and printed in Great Britain by
Unwin Brothers Limited, The Gresham Press,
Old Woking, Surrey
for Ian Henry Publications, Ltd.
38 Parkstone Avenue, Hornchurch, Essex, RM11 3LW

TO MY WIFE

TO JENNIFER

AND TO JULIA WHO CANNOT

YET READ

FOREWORD TO THE SECOND EDITION

Archie White, who died in 1957 at the wretchedly early age of 58, has left indelible memories with all those who knew him as artist, as yachtsman and as personality.

His marine water colours are altogether too little known and too little appreciated, despite a memorable retrospective exhibition held in Colchester in 1975. They are marvellously fluent and accomplished. He was a master of oil painting as well, but he never thought so much of this easier and more popular medium, which he characteristically called 'pudding painting'. And when one looks at his seas and skies, his ships and their rigging, recorded for ever in the swift, authoritative strokes of his water colour brushes, which had to get it exactly right first time, and did, one can understand his preference.

As a yachtsman he belonged to and epitomised a Corinthian period—the golden age of the Little Ship Club and his own Narrow Seas Club. He was not interested in racing, but liked to go to sea to make long passages to faraway places. He told us of the younger generation always to take a fair wind and then to trust providence for a fair wind home again. If you slogged away to windward the chance was that the wind would change and you could slog all the way home again, he would explain. He once set off for a holiday cruise to the Baltic when easterly weather set in, so he said to his crew 'We've got all the English Channel charts aboard; let's put the helm up and have a look at the Channel Islands instead'. Which they did, and then ran back at the end of the holiday before a sou'westerly.

Of course, his old gaff cutter *Acushla*, and after her the yawl *Concord*, built for him at Pin Mill, would not go to windward like the offshore cruiser-racers of today, but this was not the reason. He had a sailor's love of rolling along before a fair wind and following sea with the boom off, relying on his compass, log and parallel rule, the navigational tools of his time.

The East Coast he knew so well and loved so much, and the Blackwater more than anywhere else, was a freer and less crowded place than it is today. The barges, oyster smacks and shrimp bawleys still sailed, the yachts were characterfully individualist products of the local boatyards, not mass-produced and sold at the Boat Show, and you could still let go your anchor in many an unspoiled corner of Essex and Suffolk and go ashore to a pub for a pint and a yarn with half a dozen local regulars.

These are the tideways and byways he describes, and rightly no attempt has been made to bring his accounts up to date—or even to correct a few factual errors which he made and which don't matter in the least.

He dedicated the first edition to 'My wife, to Jennifer and to Julia, who cannot yet read.' Mrs White still lives in the wooden bungalow which Archie had built at West Mersea, and both his daughters have now taught their own children to read. It all seems a long time ago, though only thirty years have passed.

And how his style is of the period! Who else would happily mark at Southend, 'A pier, it would appear', or label a lightship as 'Knock John on the Boko'? This is writing without inhibitions, yarning fancy free. Those who knew him will hear the author's voice again, telling tall tales and making outrageous jokes with the Essex pronunciation which he liked to exaggerate a little to confuse excessively polite and genteel company.

Those who didn't know him will find a picture of an easier and more spacious age and a lovable character who was part of it.

West Mersea, 1977   Hervey Benham

CONTENTS

ILLUSTRATIONS

MAPS AND CHARTS

CHAPTER I

THE LONDON RIVER

In the doldrums now we be;
Old England makes no headway.
The King spends more than is his due
The Dutch are in the Medway.

Lament of the Poor Apprentice

THE Southend Arterial Road might be described as 'a slice of life' —or death. Before the war it was a case of every man for himself and the ambulance took the casualties. An affair of the quick and the dead. Cyclists and lorries, private cars and charabancs hurtled every day, and every week-end in particular, along that dull, uninteresting highway. The charabancs especially hurtled. Invulnerable owing to size and weight they bore within themselves an hilarious crowd. Cockneys all! Good-hearted, lavish with money, vulgar but extremely happy, they swarmed into wayside inns built specially for fleeting accommodation, drank heartily and swiftly, reboarded their juggernauts the merrier for refreshment and continued their way to the sea. At eventide after a full day they returned, full of song, full of beer and as stewed as the eels with which favourite dish they had supported life since the morning. They were, as the saying goes, 'all alive'. My young cousin used to be fond of telling a story about a fishmonger who was also a lay-preacher. His discourses were original and popular, but enthusiasm became uncontrolled when he finished a particularly stimulating sermon with 'and save your souls alive!—all alive O!! all alive!!!'

No doubt the 'arterial' scene will be re-created and Southend regain her popularity. Having once taken an unwilling part in this fight for life (escaping whole) and preferring now to contemplate the

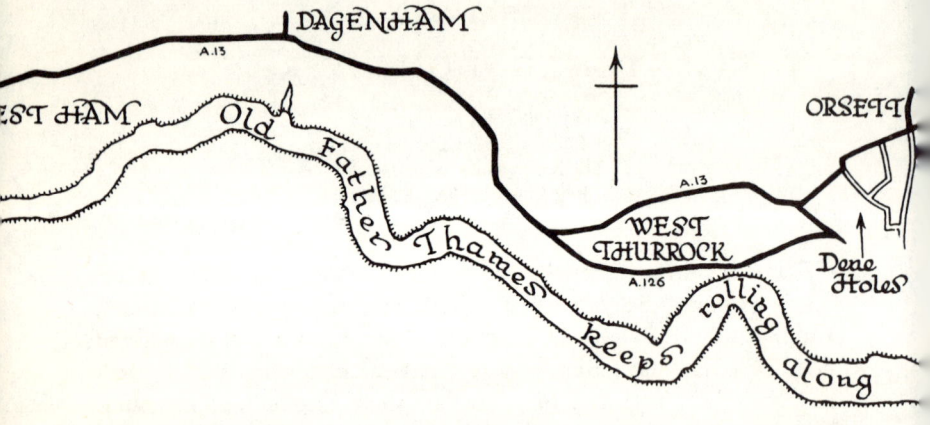

excitement in retrospect, I find that the comparative quiet of the Old Southend Road appeals. Fork left past Dagenham, bear left again before coming to Stanford-le-Hope (where Joseph Conrad lived) and carry on through Vange and Pitsea, or, if you feel in a mind to have a look at the 'Dene Holes' at East Thurrock, you will find them in Hangman's Wood to the east of the road near Orsett Heath. They consist of many shafts, three or four feet wide, going straight down eighty feet or so into chalk. All Dene Holes go down to chalk. At the bottom are rooms or chambers, several to each shaft, about twenty feet square and twelve or fourteen feet high. Although called 'Dane Holes' locally they have nothing to do with the Danes but are of Celtic origin, so the experts tell us. But the experts cannot tell us why Dene Holes were made. No one can. Some believe them to be merely chalk pits. But why should the Celts go to the immense labour of digging so far down for chalk which could be obtained in abundance

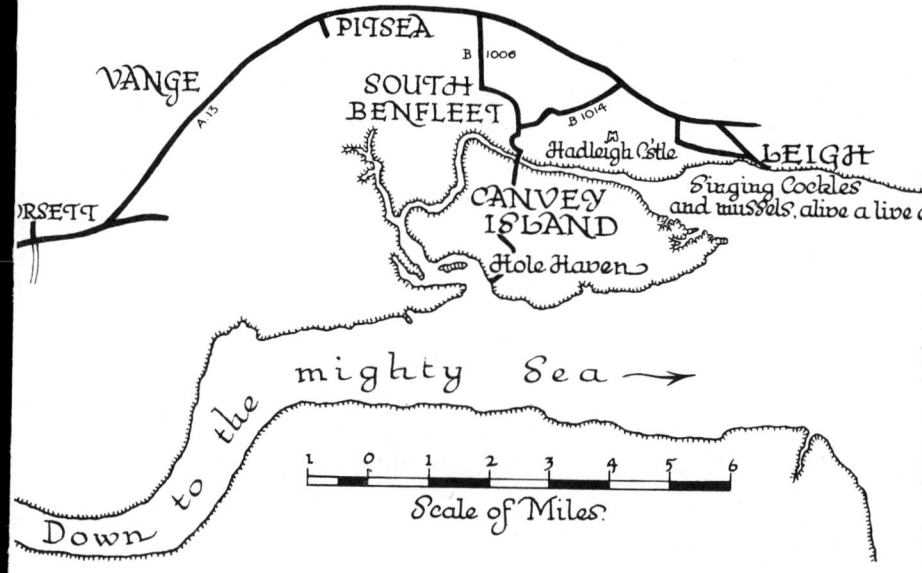

near, or on, the surface? Why should the holes be all about the same size, and why dig about seventy? 'Ah,' says another school of thought, 'they were used by a tribe as places of refuge from wild beasts and invaders.' Self-preservation was paramount in Celtic times just as it is to-day. It is hardly likely therefore that a terrified people would descend into the bowels of the earth to escape from a wolf whose coat they needed nor from an enemy whom they feared. They would have to lower a store of food and water. They could never defeat an adversary since they could never attack him, nor would they have any means of defence. Piecemeal annihilation or starvation would be the alternative facing them, neither very inviting. They would indeed be in a 'hole'. Some thinkers assert that Dene Holes have a religious significance—that a sect worshipped down below or fled in dread and terror from their gods—the gods of the wind and the rain, of the sun and the moon—the gods of thunder and lightning. But, if these

15

people crouched before the fury of the storm, they did so under trees and not under ground; if they worshipped the sun and the moon they did so with those gods looking down upon them.

A mile and a half beyond Pitsea turn right for South Benfleet, cross

the bridge over the Creek and you are on Canvey Island. In the dim ages the island resembled a swamp, intersected, divided and cut about by innumerable creeks and gullies. The spring tides almost submerged it. Those few who lived there ploughed up the clay with their primitive ploughs or ploughed up the muddy foreshore with their primitive feet in search of whelks, cockles, periwinkles and other shellfish. Some ventured in crazy craft upon the muddy river to catch fish. The meagre harvest from land and sea would be taken upstream to the settlement at London and there bartered for goods to be had only in a town. There they would hear tales of how the Romans had been upsetting the peace of the southern part of the country and had since gone away. Consequently when they saw triremes pass up-river, their banks of oars rising and falling methodically, watchers on Canvey would understand and know that the Romans had come again. The wide, low, soft, yielding mud protected the islanders from the invader. With his ships anchored far away in the stream, with his heavy armour weighing him down as he floundered through the ooze, the Roman would have been no match for the British slings and arrows.

The great galleys therefore went farther up-stream to stay the night at a bend in the river where a deep channel scoured near to a hard foreshore convenient for anchoring to remain afloat, or handy for beaching and getting away again. Up to ninety or a hundred feet in length, these galleys amounted to great rowing-boats filled with soldiers. They had a square sail hoisted athwart-ships to help them forward when the wind served, but there was little 'sailorizing' and the art of 'tacking' was not at all understood. The Romans were better lawyers than sailors, and such of their ships as traded in the Mediterranean were manned principally by Greeks. Our rules relating to the insurance of ships and cargoes are based upon Roman usage. They hit upon the plan, which is followed to-day, of insuring the ship and her cargo separately. It sometimes happens that a cargo is jettisoned in order to save the ship. On other occasions the vessel itself might be beached to save the cargo.

If by chance you meet a man who describes himself as an 'average adjuster', don't for a moment think that he sits in a newspaper office at the close of a warm summer's day working in decimals, the fruits of which labour you see the next morning in the batting and bowling averages. No: 'average adjusters' are people employed by cargo-owners and shipowners to assess the proper proportion each party should be called upon to pay in cases of the deliberate stranding of a ship or of the purposeful jettisoning of a cargo.

The tide-sodden Canvey watched the Romans come and go, saw

the Saxons and Danes arrive. These invasions, extending over a thousand years, left no mark, and it is not until Queen Elizabeth is said to have visited the island after reviewing her troops at East Tilbury in 1588 that history is made again.

The 'Lobster Smack' mentioned in Dickens's *Great Expectations* was in Elizabethan times a modern inn, condemned, no doubt, by the older inhabitants as a new-fangled upstart. One of those old codgers, seeing 'Gloriana', might have remembered how, when a boy, he saw the *Henri Grace a Dieu*—the Great Harry—that most remarkable of all Tudor ships, with her tremendous streamers and magnificent banners floating in the breeze, her tall upper works decorated, painted and gilded as no other ship had ever been before, shining in the

THE LOBSTER SMACK. CANVEY ISLAND

OLD DUTCH HOUSE, CANVEY ISLAND

afternoon sun, her musicians playing martial music as she slipped down the river on her maiden voyage out to sea.

In 1622 Canvey was changed from a semi-morass into dry land when Dutchmen, headed by one named Coppenburgh, built a dike, or wall, round the island. How well they wrought can be seen to-day. The island produced crops and became famous for the fattening of cattle. Prosperity arrived, and Saturday nights at the now fairly established 'Lobster Smack' were no doubt something to remember as the monied Dutchmen came in for their pints and sang their boisterous and outlandish songs. Forty-five years later they came again, this time not to construct but to destroy. Landing on the island they harried the people, drove away cattle and set fire to the church. The English fleet openly threatened to join the invaders, a not altogether astonishing circumstance since they were seldom paid. Andrew Marvell in his *Instructions to a Painter,* says

> Our seamen, whom no dangers shape can fright,
> Unpaid, refuse to mount their ships for spite.
> Or, to their fellows swim on board the Dutch
> Who shew them tempting metal in their clutch.

The Netherlanders patrolled the east coast from Lowestoft to the Straits. They entered the Medway, 'cutting out' several of His Majesty's ships (notably the *Royal Charles*) from under the guns of Upnor Castle. They sailed up the Thames as far as the Lower Hope; the confusion afloat was equalled by the chaotic state of affairs ashore.

Samuel Pepys, at that time Secretary to the Admiralty, was at his wits' end, not only how to provide food and money for his beloved navy, but also on account of his personal fortune. Let him tell his vivid tale.

June 13th, 1667. I presently resolved of my father's and wife's going into the country; and, at two hours' warning, they did go by the coach this day, with about £1,300 in gold in their night-bag. Pray God give them good passage, and good care to hide it when they come home, but my heart is full of fear. . . . I did, about noon, resolve to send Mr. Gibson away after my wife with another 1,000 pieces. . . . I also sent, my mind being in pain, Saunders after my wife and father, to overtake them at their night's lodgings to see how matters go with

them. . . . I have also made a girdle, by which, with some trouble, I do carry about me £300 in gold about my body, that I may not be without something in case I am surprised.

June 15th. At night comes, unexpectedly so soon, Mr. Gibson, who left my wife well, and all got down well with them, but not with himself, which I was afraid of, and cannot blame him, but must myself be wiser against another time. He had one of his bags broke, through his breeches, and some pieces dropped out, not many he thinks, but two, for he light, and took them up, and went back and could find no more. But I am not able to tell how many, which troubles me, but the joy of having the greatest part safe there makes me bear with it. Home, and to my flageolet.

June 19th. My wife did give so bad an account of her and my father's method in burying of our gold, that made me mad: and she herself is not pleased with it, she believing that my sister knows of it. **My father and she did it on Sunday, when they were gone to church, in open daylight,** in the midst of the garden; where, for aught they knew, many eyes might see them: which put me into trouble, and I presently cast about, how to have it back again, to secure it here, the times being a little better now.

On August 9th, 1667, peace was signed between England and Holland, and our friend lost no time in recovering his hidden gold. Taking coach to Brampton in Huntingdonshire where the hoard had been deposited, on August 10th, he records, 'My father and I with a dark lantern, it being now night, into the garden with my wife, and there went about our great work to dig up my gold. But Lord! what a tosse I was for some time in, that they could not justly tell where it was; that I begun heartily to sweat, and be angry . . . but by and by poking with a spit, we found it and then began with a spudd to lift up the ground. But, good God! to see how sillily they did it, not half a foot under ground, and in the sight of the world from a hundred places. . . . I was out of my wits almost, and the more from that, upon my

lifting the earth with the spudd, I did discern that
I had scattered the pieces of gold round about the
ground among the grass and loose earth; and taking
up the iron head-pieces wherein they were put, I
perceived the earth was got among the gold, and wet,
so that the bags were all rotten, and all the notes,
that I could not tell what in the world to say to it,
not knowing how to judge what was wanting, which,
all put together, did made me mad; and at last I was
able to take up the head-pieces, dirt and all, and as
many of the scattered pieces as I could with the dirt
discern by candle-light, and carry them up into my
brother's chamber, and there locke them up till I had
eat a little supper: and then, all people going to bed,
W. Hewer and I did all alone, with several pails of
water and besoms, at the last wash the dirt off of the
pieces . . . and do find that there was short above a
hundred pieces: which did make me mad. . . . Hewer
and I out again about midnight, for it was now

grown so late, and there by candle-light did make shift to gather forty-five pieces more. And so in, and to cleanse them: and by this time it was past two in the morning; and so to bed with my mind pretty quiet to think that I have recovered so many.'

There you have an intimate picture of the effect the Dutch had on at least one man living at the time. To touch Pepys's purse was to make of him a craven, to touch his honour was to make him a lion, as was amply shown when he remained at his post throughout the dreadful plague when other men fled to hoped-for safety.

So history passes from Canvey, unless we include boxing. In the last century many notable 'mills' took place, and it is said that the great Tom Sayers and Heenan fought forty-eight rounds on the green-sward outside the 'Lobster Smack'.

To stand on the sea-wall and watch the ships of the world go by is an experience. Great liners, racing up Sea Reach to save the tide at Tilbury Docks, or farther up, send the buoys all a-bobbing and a-ringing as the wash astern comes tumbling noisily along the muddy banks. Dutchmen standing at their horizontal wheels like tram-drivers, 'chonk-chonk' up river. Oil tankers, freighters, tramps; timber-ships (called 'Onkers') from the Baltic, listing over as they come; tugs towing hoppers on immensely long wires take advantage of the tide. Then there are the barges. To watch a barge tacking up-river with a spring tide in a smart breeze of a wind is a sight to see. Unless you knew the power of the tide you would think she must inevitably hit a buoy, but no—she is carried on far beyond it until the edge of the mud is almost reached. The steersman turns his iron wheel and the barge's huge staysail becomes limp. But only for a moment. Tremendous booms, like the discharge of guns afar off, sound across the river as the mighty sail flacks head to wind. The topsail, seen edge on, becomes to all appearances thin, like a handkerchief. But not for long. Soon the noise is augmented by the mainsail as it swings to and fro on its gigantic sprit. The mizzen, which is attached to the rudder, also moves over from one side to the other but in sedate fashion, like a foreman

24

watching to see that everything 'forrard' is properly done—as though it had charge of everything and was not to be hustled. The barge swings round catching as she turns a dollop of sparkling water rainbowed in the sun at her bows. The staysail, now all aback and shoving mightily, is let fly. The wind, filling the great brown canvas sails, sets them once again into those lovely, lovely curves as the vessel, healing a little now, gathers way, and is off on the other tack.

Smallest of all craft on this most famous of rivers are the yachts. Charles the First (or rather the Dutch who gave him a yacht to play with) started the fashion in this country. In those spacious days the only way of getting along on the water was by sail or oar. Now, to steer a yacht on the London river is a question, not of giving way to some, or taking precedence over others, but of giving way to all. In theory a sailing vessel has the right of way over steam. In practice it is wise to avoid anything bigger than yourself if you are able to do so. Even in Hole Haven, the Canvey Island anchorage for yachts and the most sheltered in the river, one has to keep a weather eye wide open because of the increasing traffic, and should you leave your vessel there during the week you must hire someone to tend it and bend on a riding light every night.

Before the age of oil and petrol the Haven used to be more popular with yachtsmen than it is to-day, but it is still a favourite rendezvous of the merry men of Erith, in whose famous clubhouse beer is poured from quart bottles only, the pint being an unknown quantity.

One can sail a small boat at high water round the island past Benfleet, coming out into the river again between Leigh and Southend Pier.

When the railway station at Benfleet was being constructed, just under the surface a tremendous quantity of burnt wood was found. This discovery corroborated the account given in the Anglo-Saxon Chronicle of a tremendous fight between the Danes and King Alfred. The Chronicle relates how Alfred, surprising the settlement, set fire to the place, doing the same to, or capturing, the Danish ships.

Hadleigh Castle on the high ground above, and toward Leigh, is worth a visit. After all, if Constable found it worth while to paint, surely such as we can find it in ourselves to ascend the hill and admire the magnificent view of the Kentish hills across the river which winds its silvery way fascinatingly down to the sea. Below, and a little farther seawards is Leigh. 'A pretty little town,' said Camden, 'stocked with lusty seamen.' From the bridge at the station one looks down upon a

A LEIGH BAWLEY

picturesque collection of roofs beneath; higgledy-piggledy, they run and leap like a scene from a Walt Disney film.

I don't suppose there is anything in England quite like the path running along the shore. The old 'Ship Inn' is there, so are the cockle-sheds, much as they were in 'Gotty's' day. Gotty was a local character whose fame spread far beyond Leigh. As a bare-fist fighter he was the equal of many policemen, as a walker of the greasy pole he had no fear, and he knew better than most the habits of cockles and swimming

26

fishes. He vindicated his claim to be a navigator triumphantly when one who should have known better said, 'Gotty! I'll bet you a florin you can't even read a compass.' 'Done,' said Gotty excitedly, banging his fist on the counter in the bar of 'The Ship'. 'Bring a compass. Now then,' says he, 'north, east, south and west, and the two bob's mine!' Only death could defeat Gotty—and then only partially— since he lives to-day in A. E. Copping's *Gotty and the Guvnor* and *Gotty in Furrin Parts*.

Besides cockle-sheds, house-boats line the road. Hundreds of them. Letter-boxes are cut into their sides, and wooden containers, suspended from wires and filled with earth, make the bottom of the garden the bottom of the box. 'No Hawkers—No Circulars' is to be seen and it is difficult to imagine that these contraptions ever swam on the water, once things of beauty and of grace.

In Elizabethan times Leigh was described as 'a very proper place where tall ships do ride'. It still is 'a very proper place', but in place of the 'tall ships' only the last of the 'bawleys' and 'cocklers' ride in the creek. A Leigh 'bawley' is a vessel generally between thirty and forty feet in length, full-bodied, with a good beam and drawing between five and a half and six and a half feet of water. They trawl for shrimps, whitebait and sprats when the proper seasons come round, and for any sort of fish they can catch when they see a chance. They are cutter-rigged with a peculiarly fashioned boomless mainsail and a very long gaff indeed. To control the mainsail, the sheet reeves through two large single blocks on the sail and is made fast to an iron pin thrust through a block on the deck. A blow from one of these iron-clad monsters as it travels viciously across the after part of the bawley's deck has been likened to the 'crack of doom'. Many descriptions have been given of the blocks themselves but none, other than those of a purely technical nature, have ever appeared in print owing to wise laws which control and make unprofitable the publication of obscenities.

The 'cocklers' as their name implies are used to gather cockles. They leave Leigh at high-water and sail as fast as they are able to their favourite fishing-grounds, the Maplin Sands. Fishing-'grounds' is literally correct. The boats are driven ashore, becoming high and dry as the tide falls. Their crews step on to the hard sand and rake into heaps as many cockles as they can before the tide returns. These they put aboard in a 'well' in the centre of the boat and hasten back to Leigh. The day when you can see dozens of bawleys and cocklers under sail is gone and will never return. The internal combustion engine has cut off the long top-mast of the bawley and stuck a flag-stick in its place. The cocklers go under engine also, which saves time and gives greater certainty. So the industry lives on. In the sheds ashore the shell fish are prepared. Big coppers filled with boiling water are fed with cockles in wire bags by descendants of Camden's 'lusty seamen'. This scalding causes the shells to open, and in a few minutes the fish are cooked. From the copper they are then spread upon large oblong shallow trays with finely meshed wire bottoms. From pipes above cold water steadily sprinkles, and the laden trays, suspended from the roof, are swung to and fro so that the whole area of cockles is cooled and cleaned of sand in a single process.

On the sides of the sheds facing the roadway, shutters hinge down to form a counter covered with white, shiny, easily cleaned American cloth upon which are displayed in little plates or saucers cockles freshly cooked, together with shrimps, prawns and other delicacies.

A large pepper-pot is handy, while a hole in the cork of a whisky bottle emits vinegar. Twopence! Very tasty! Tons of cockles (and I means tons) are sent to London, and a great quantity goes to nearby Southend. How many tons of shells there are accumulated in the vast heaps on the foreshore is difficult to estimate. Now and again a barge takes a load away. Lorries remove a quantity from time to time. Where they all go to is a mystery. Where they all come from is a mystery too.

'Yes,' said one old fisherman as I seasoned my two-pennyworth, 'what we wants is a lot o' sun and bands.' 'What sort of bands?'

'Oh! Any sort of band'll do—string or brass—that's all one to me—but let's hev 'um—with plenty o' sunshine, then we shall all be happy!'

What about the smell? Yes—perhaps there is just the faintest trace of an odour hanging about the place, which might be due to the boiling of cockles. 'But Lor' bless ye,' as my old band and sunshine loving friend said, 'yew don't want to take no notice o' that.' Go down to Leigh therefore, take a look round and chat with one of the fishermen and you'll have a tale worth telling when you go to the office on Monday morning.

Lower down the river is Southend, of which nothing need be said here except that the approach to the sea is by way of the pier.

COCKLERS.

CHAPTER II

THE ROACH

Mushrooms he ate, both cooked and raw
Upon his holiday.

ANON

COMING down from Southend Pier in a yacht bound for the Roach and Crouch an opportunity is afforded to measure the speed of the vessel. On the edge of the Maplin Sands off Shoeburyness the Admiralty have set up two pairs of beacons which are a sea-mile apart.

I have yet to hear of a yachtsman taking times between the posts when beating against the tide, but, after all, under such conditions the information is of service only to an enemy and is best left ungarnered.

To do the job properly and with credit to all concerned it is best to have a spring tide in your favour together with a nice fair wind. Incredible speeds may then be achieved and the record of them, if believed, is of value, when it comes to selling the boat.

With a foul wind, getting out of the London river in a sailing craft is a difficult business. It is useless to start with not enough wind, while a hard breeze soon knocks up a short, steep, vicious sea in the Swin, and headway, if any, is slow and uncomfortable.

It takes a fast and weatherly vessel to beat from Sea Reach down to Harwich on a tide, and if she cannot save it there is precious little shelter to be had unless she runs for the Crouch or the Colne.

With an easterly wind of some days' duration you will find the Medway crowded with barges waiting for a 'slant'. Days and days and days of irritating and unprofitable idleness. But, one day, the

30

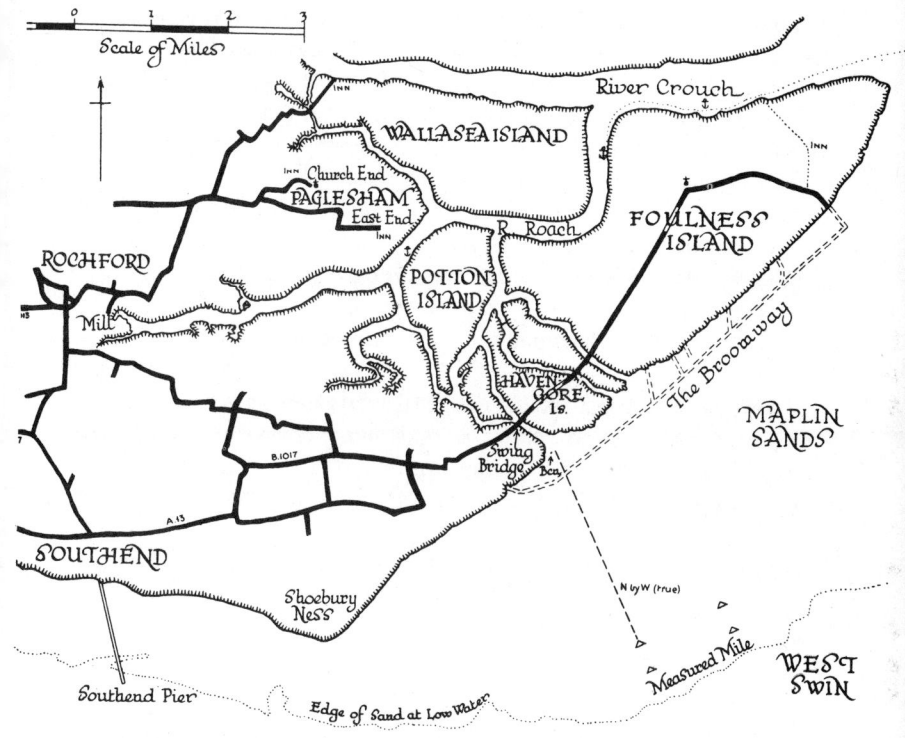

Scale of Miles

River Crouch

WALLASEA ISLAND

Church End

PAGLESHAM
East End

R. Roach

FOULNESS
ISLAND

ROCHFORD

POTTON
ISLAND

Mill

The Broomway

HAVEN
GORE
Is.

MAPLIN
SANDS

B.1017

Swing
Bridge   Bcn

A 13

SOUTHEND

Shoebury
Ness

N by W (true)

Measured Mile

WEST
SWIN

Southend Pier

Edge of Sand at Low Water

'bob', as the flag or pennant is called, ripples in another direction at the tall top-mast head. No matter at what hour comes the moment when that 'bob' slews round, that is also the moment when every barge skipper's eye is fixed upon it. The merry 'clank clank clank— clank clank clank' of the windlass pawls is heard at once as cables are shortened. Topsails climb up slowly and, with the setting of the staysail and the unbrailing of the main, the fleet gets under way and out of sight within the hour.

There came a day after one such spell of easterly weather when it so

31

happened that, seen from the Spitway Buoy, the horizon became pitted with dots. Turning into triangles as they advanced, they resolved themselves at last into barges. A whole string of them there were. Over a score. A sight not seen every day of the week. They came down-Swin in a long line with as much precision as a platoon of well trained infantrymen in open order.

As they approached, a mighty roar of water came from the bluff bows thrusting the seas aside. So near were they that we could hear the song of the wind in the rigging supporting the mast, could hear the breeze pressing against those towering pillars of canvas. Each bargee raised his hand from his iron wheel to wave as he thundered past.

After the prolonged spell of the pestilential easterlies the warm, moist south-west wind acted like a balm, reviving the spirit. It sent the barges triumphantly on their way, ramping along, stamping down the water, to haul their sheets for a short hitch as they marched through

the Spitway, easing them again a trifle to bear away through the Wallet bound down to Harwich.

A shaft of sunlight covered them with glory. Twenty-four of them there were that day; long may such sights delight the eyes and gladden the hearts of those of us who love to see a ship sailing upon the sea.

When the art of tacking was unknown and the use of fore and aft sails a mystery, vessels had even greater difficulty than now in getting beyond the Swin. Take as an instance the voyage of the *Speranza* in

33

2

1553 as recorded by Hakluyt. She was 'a shippe of 150 tunnes', under the command of Sir Hugh Willoughby, and the voyage was under-taken to discover Cathay.

The venture came to a sad end, Sir Hugh and all his company being frozen to death while wintering in 'Lappia'.

Leaving Deptford on May 11th, they got no farther than 'Hollie Haven' by the 22nd. 'The 23rd day from Hollie Haven till we came against Lee and there remained that night by reason that the wind was contrary to us.' Five miles in a day!

'The 24th day the wind being in the south-west in the morning we sailed along the coast, over the Spits until we came against St. Osyth about sixe of the clocke at night.'

Even with a fair wind they took the best part of the day to run along the coast from Leigh to St. Osyth, a matter, in those days, of five and twenty miles.

By the 26th they were 'at Orwell'; by the end of the month as far north as Yarmouth. Clear of the sands now, pretty well, eh? Let's see.

'Then the last day of May into the sea sixe leagues North East and there taryd that night, when the wind blew very sore. The 1st of June the winde being at North contrary to us, we came backe againe to Orwell, and remained there untill the 15th day, tarying for the winde for all this time the winde was contrary to our purpose.' They made two or three further attempts, getting past Orfordness on one occasion but always having to run back in the end to Orwell. Not until the 23rd of June were they able finally to get away clear of everything down to the north. They took, therefore, a matter of forty-three days to get from Depford clear of Harwich. Later on in the narrative we read 'the winde veared to the West, so that we could lie but North and by West', clearly showing how poorly these old-time vessels 'pointed'.

The lowlying shore bounding the Swin is protected from the fury of the sea by the very extensive Maplin Sands. They are submerged only about four feet at H.W. Springs and are as flat as a billiard-table.

The land between Southend and the River Crouch is cut by the small Havengore Creek, which is navigable to small craft, by New England Creek which is not, and by Shelford Creek which, joining the Roach, forms Foulness Island. A queer place, recalling Erskine Childers' famous novel. No yachtsman ever turns in without reading a page or two of *The Riddle of the Sands*, but to the general public the book is not so well known as it might be. The country of Childers' tale of espionage is the Frisian Islands straggling along the German coast. The scene might well have been these Essex shores. Here are the same mysterious creeks and 'watersheds'. Here is the 'Broomway'. Here are the vast expanses of mud uncovered at low water.

As you come along the road from Southend to Foulness Island a policeman will step out from his little cottage to ask politely for your permit. No pass—no pass! At least along the military road. But he may tell you that you can take the road to the right, and although it is rough and winding it is worth the effort. Why? Because it seems to lead nowhere. To take a road leading nowhere is intriguing if only for the sake of trying to find out why the road to nowhere was ever built. Jog along over the small bridges spanning dikes and ditches till you come to a sharpish rise.

Through the opening in the sea-wall there is the sea or the vast expanse of the Maplin Sands. If the tide is low you will see something like my little sketch.

When I sat down to make the drawing a military policeman very

THE ROAD TO NOWHERE

soon came along to see what I was about, but he agreed that the picture would be of little use to an enemy. The 'Broomway', as the track is called, is the ancient, and was at one time the only, road to Foulness. At Wakering Stairs, where we now are, the road across the sands was marked on either side with 'withies' or 'brooms', tall and upstanding. To-day only the stumps are to be seen, winding their way across the mud flats to disappear in the distance.

When I was there last a great six-wheeled lorry stopped to fit caterpillars. Then, when all was ready, off she went over the sea-wall to the sands, curving this way and that, keeping to the guiding marks on either side. Her machinery rumbled in the still afternoon air long

STAMBRIDGE MILL

after she had been swallowed up by the mist. She disappeared into a void.

The 'Broomway' itself is hard, but leave the track and you will soon be in a pocket of softness. Tales have been told of horses and carts becoming engulfed in the treacherous sands to perish as the tide came in; how years ago the Foulness parson had a narrow escape. But then tales always have been told.

My cousin used to tell of long ago when Foulness was inhabited only by sea-birds and a sparse population, as indeed it is to-day. A medical man visited the island to inquire into the state of the health of the inhabitants. 'How do you manage without a doctor?' he asked. 'Why, Lor' bless y', Sir' said an old man, 'we dies of ourselves.'

The river Roach, branching off from the Crouch, is tidal as far as picturesque Great Stambridge Mill. Its muddy banks make for safety and one may anchor almost anywhere, though in Paglesham Reach the holding ground is said not to be wonderfully good, the mud being 'thinner'. Off Paglesham itself the trees in the background, contrast-ing with the flat land all round, make it a pleasant place at which to lie at anchor, the more so as Mr. Shuttlewood has lately made an excellent hard upon which one can land cleanly.

To get ashore or afloat water boots are essential. This state of affairs led a city man to invent soluble water boots to be pulled on over ordinary shoes. After being immersed for some time they slowly dissolved, leaving the wearer, now safely on dry land, in his shore-going shoes. But the idea never took on.

The hardy (and handy) men who use Paglesham as a base for their yachting activities have little sheds or cabins ashore in which to store their gear and work. I was going to say they did all the work themselves but this would be a libel on Frank Shuttlewood who does some too. The results of his labours are to be seen (and admired) on the river. They tell me a bad boat has never yet been launched from his yard, certainly a badly built one never has. But at heart he is a barge-man and, I believe, would like more than anything to build an old-time wooden 'spritty'. If he knows you well he may let you look at a model of one he has built, a fine affair, correct in every detail. Models are nice things to have about the house, especially if they are of one's own yacht. A great deal of patience and skill goes into a really good, planked-up replica and the work is sometimes a bit beyond every Tom, Dick or Harry. But all three should be able to put a model into a bottle and this is how it is done.

First of all make plans of the yacht scaled down sufficiently for the hull to pass through the neck, which is usually three-quarters of an inch across. Take care to measure the height inside the bottle for, having successfully inserted the hull, there is a tendency to irritation on finding the mast too tall to stand upright.

Square up a nice piece of straight-grained soft wood, transfer the deck plan and profile from the plan and carve the hull to a little below the water line, smoothing down finally with very fine sandpaper.

Turning it upside down gouge out fairly deep slots, one each side in

way of the rigging and back-stays. Make a fair-sized hole, but not right through, at the bow. The purpose of these hackings will be seen later.

A piece from the lid of a rich uncle's cigar-box makes admirable cabin-tops and hatch-covers when seccotined to the deck, whose

SEAWALL
PAGLESHAM

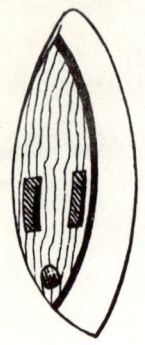

planking is suggested by thin precise lines drawn with a very sharp and very hard pencil. If the yacht has a bowsprit now is the time to whittle away a match, smooth it down and glue it in position. The model is now ready for painting. Buy artists' oil colours in tubes. They are much finer than the ordinary house paint and cheaper. The two or three tubes of the various colours required are ample for scores of models at a cost of but a few pence against shillings for gallons and gallons of inferior paint. As one proceeds with the sails and rigging, one can dab a coat of paint on the topsides, leaving it to dry without hindering the work. Finally, a couple of coats of very thin varnish over the whole makes all the difference and is well worth doing.

So much for the hull. Now for the sails and rigging. Whittle down a piece of pine for the mast, measuring the height carefully. All models depend upon scale if they are to look convincing; one too often sees clumsy-looking masts and spars. It is obviously impossible to get everything in relative proportion, but the nearer one gets to the impossible the better. Don't be afraid therefore of fining down. Selected matches are usually large enough for gaff and boom. The sails can be made from tracing cloth which has been boiled to take out the dressing. It takes colour very well and a single thin coat of seccotine is just sufficient to allow them to retain their shape should you wish for curved sails. If the mainsail is loose-footed a strand of cotton may be glued to the foot and tipped to the boom, or a thread or two of the tracing cloth left at the leach answers the same purpose. But, if it is to resemble a laced sail, then we must treat it as we shall the gaff.

Cut the sail too long in the hoist but mark the position and angle of the peak and foot. With a safety-razor blade split the gaff almost to the peak and the boom almost to its outward end. Give the inside surfaces a thin coat of seccotine. Slide the sail between them at the

40

proper angles and press the wood together. At the same time push a piece of fuse wire length-wise into the inner ends of the two spars leaving an inch or two protruding.

When thoroughly dry the head and foot can be trimmed off neatly with old friend razor blade and our sail is ready for the mast. To force the piece of fuse wire on the gaff fore and aft through the mast at the hounds with a small pair of nippers is easier than it sounds. Do the same with the boom. Snip off the ends fairly short, and bend over into the mast itself. We now have two quite strong hinges which will allow us to fold the sail along the mast when the time comes to shove the model into the bottle and which will also enable us to trim the sails when they are in.

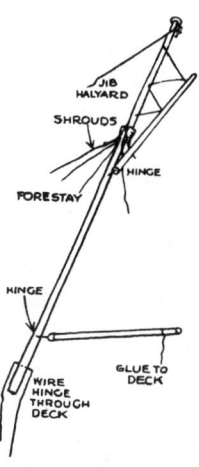

There are two ways of dealing with the mast. It may be split at the heel and a piece of thread inserted and glued. Pass the thread into a hole bored with a needle through the hull, leaving plenty of end to reach out through the neck of the bottle. When the mast is raised the thread can be kept taut or nearly so, thus guiding and holding the mast in position.

Another way is to thrust a rather stouter piece of fuse wire athwart-ships through the mast about an eighth of an inch above the heel. The two ends are then led through needle-holes in the hull and bent over underneath. Thus a fore and aft hinge is made. The staysail and jib may now be cut to shape; a piece of very fine cotton, tipped with seccotine laid along the luffs (to port, mind!) form the luff ropes, which can be either turned round the mast in their appropriate positions and glued, or passed through the mast itself with a needle and knotted on the after side.

Through the mast is better, I think, and remember to leave plenty of

41

'spare' at the foot because the end must reach out through the mouth of the bottle.

We may now beeswax pieces of cotton which smooths them and helps them to 'run'. Tip the peak halyards in position on the gaff with glue and make fast as described for the foresail. Make the hinge for the mast and set it up. The rigging, of slightly stouter cotton or thread, should now be given an overhead turn at the hounds and the ends, two or more on each side, passed through the deck at the chain plates with a needle. Similarly with the backstays. The sense of the grooves will now be apparent, as the needle will pass easily through the deck.

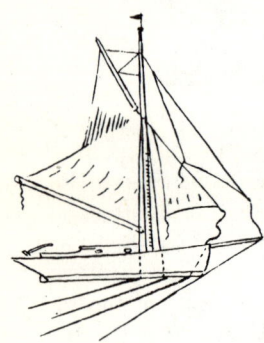

See that the mast is upright, tighten up the shrouds on either side, gluing them in the grooves underneath. Spreaders, made of cut pins, may be fitted with stays led through the deck in the same way as the rigging. Light boards made of cardboard glued to the shrouds lend a nice touch of colour to our little model which is now looking 'something like'.

Reeve the forestay through the deck at the stem and pass the luff of the jib through an eye in a piece of fuse wire which has been thrust into the bowsprit end. Cut a little notch in the forefoot to take this luff which acts as a bobstay and also as an additional mast support.

Jib and foresail sheets of

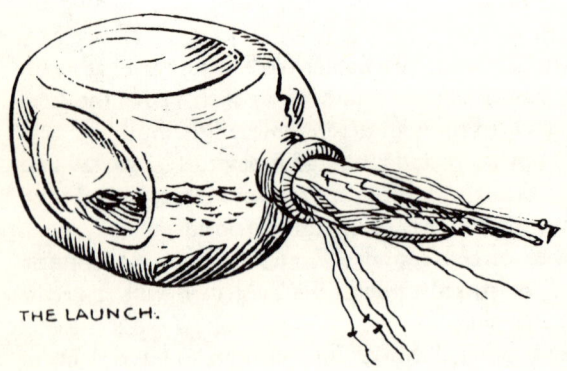

THE LAUNCH.

42

cotton may now be tipped to their respective sails and led to their proper places on deck. Similarly with the main-sheet. We are now ready to fill the bottle, the emptying of which has been so pleasant. 'Dimple' bottles are intriguing and are, I think, best of all, but the square bottles which they tell me contained gin are very useful, being better than the ordinary round variety which require some sort of stand to save them from rolling about.

Get the inside of the bottle perfectly clean and dry. Our sea is made with whiting and linseed oil and coloured, or with gland packing, which I think is better. It is easily moulded when warmed and takes colour well; mixed with soot from a chimney it admirably suggests those cold grey seas so familiar to us week-end summer yachtsmen. With a piece of bent wood enter the substance, a little at a time, pressing it down firmly, building up and moulding the waves as desired. Take care to keep the sides of the bottle clean as it is almost impossible to take out any 'mistakes'; but the inevitable mess round the neck can easily be wiped away with a cloth round the little finger.

Laying the mast and sails horizontally along the deck, push the model head first into the bottle, guiding and pressing her down to her marks with a piece of wood which can then be used to give the mast a 'start'. Haul away on the end of the forestay until the mast is upright, tightening up the jib at the same time. Cut off the two ends as far in the bottle as you can with your wife's nail scissors and bury them (the ends—not the scissors) for ever beneath the waves.

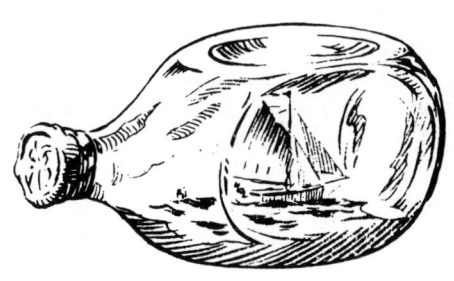

COMPLETELY BOTTLED

Set up the peak and pay off the mainsail with

43

a knitting needle and the model is finished except for corking. A coat of varnish round the cork makes an air-tight job, a generous blob of sealing-wax impressed with one's armorial bearings looks brave, while a piece of baize from a friend's billiard-table glued to the base saves the grand piano.

PAGLESHAM

But we must get back to that pretty little lane at Paglesham which leads from the hard to the 'Plough and Sail' where 'launch suppers' are eaten and where the 'phut' of the dart is heard in the bar. The talk is all of yachts and the sea. The history and attainments of every local vessel are known but, however well established the facts may be, there seems always plenty of room for healthy argument.

There are two Pagleshams (a charming name), East End and Church End. Yachts are unknown at Church End, the talk there being of crops. No sooner had I sat myself down in a hedge to make a drawing than a man came along who I could see was suspicious of my movements, or lack of them. It turned out he was afraid I was 'after his bees'. I was afraid his bees were after me. He kindly invited me in to look at his charming farm-house, full of treasures.

44

Later, over a pint, I listened to words of wisdom about pigs; there was nothing for it but to visit the sties, albeit we had to stand a little way off; the pigs were young and the parent tended to fierceness if upset.

These chance meetings are delightful and should be encouraged. I don't mean to say one should career round the countryside pestering people to show you their houses, but I do say that wherever one goes there is always someone ready to talk of the things which interest him and who is very likely a master of his craft. One can learn something then. Such an one I met whose life seemed dedicated to potatoes. He measured what he called 'a parcel of ground' with his mind's eye, inwardly computing the quantity it would yield. He examined potatoes carefully; after hearing him talk I examined them carefully too. For weeks after the meeting at meal-times the potato loomed large on the table. Its size, its shape, its mealiness, its colour, all were solemnly discussed. We became for the time being, connoisseurs. 'After all,' as he said, 'take away 'taters and where are you?'

On your way to Paglesham you will very likely have passed through Rochford, a busy little place on market days, full of interest and bustle.

Here the famous 'Lawless Court' was held annually on the Wednesday preceding Michaelmas before 'the first cock-crowing'. This meant that the proceedings were held in the dark. The Steward would call the name of a tenant in so low a voice that the unfortunate man, unable to hear and give an answer, would thereupon be sharply fined. The tenants also spoke in a whisper and records were kept in charcoal.

The 'Court' was held under the stars just outside the town. How, or for what purpose the curious custom started is not known. The last 'Court' took place in 1868.

Before we leave the Roach a word must be said about Wallasea Island. Having no parish church it yet has five, the area being divided among that number of adjoining parishes. It has the smallest school in Essex, the number of scholars rarely exceeding six. Which led the late Sir W. Gurney Benham to remark that although the number of classes was uncertain 'it may be taken for granted that there is an upper and a lower sixth'.

The island was long famous for the quality of its oysters—the Romans called them 'Wallfleets'. 'A full little oyster,' Norden said, 'with a verie greene fyne, and like unto this in qualitie and quantitie are none in these lands.' There is Defoe's comment, 'On this shoar also are taken the best and nicest, tho' not the largest oysters in England.'

I am convinced that the Wallet, that channel now running along the Essex coast past Clacton, takes its name from Wallasea Island, from which it flowed in ancient times. Besides oysters, the island is renowned for its mushrooms. I know a yachtsman who always takes his holiday late in the year when they are in season. As soon as it is light, and before the warm September mists have cleared (there's a reason for this!) off he goes ashore from his yacht to gather a bag full of his favourite dish. For a whole fortnight he subsists on nothing but mushrooms. Enormous quantities of them. Mushrooms fried, mushrooms boiled in milk, in pies, and mushrooms raw. Any and all ways he eats them and, apart from a blackened tongue, seems none the worse.

CHAPTER III

THE CROUCH

And warlike weapons, now consumed with cank'ring rust
The huge and mossy bones of mighty fearful men,
To tell the world's full strength what creatures lived then,
When in her height of youth the lusty fruitful earth
Brought forth her big limbed brood, even giants in their birth.

DRAYTON. *Polyolbion*

FROM Shore Ends at its mouth to Battlesbridge, where it ceases to be navigable, the River Crouch runs pretty well east and west for fifteen miles. Between its not very extensive mud banks the stream flows fairly and strongly, at least for an East Coast river. It becomes fiercer from Creeksea Ferry downwards, the river having then to carry water from off the marshes. Except at Burnham, which we shall come to in a minute, one can bring up in safety almost anywhere. When the wind comes from the south-west a very good anchorage is provided at the mouth of the river in the lee of Foulness Island with good holding ground. When the wind comes in easterly it is best to nip round the corner into the Roach, two and a half miles or so above Shore Ends. A newly married couple once spent their entire fortnight's honeymoon there, so quiet and undisturbed is the anchorage—and the wind holding in the east.

The only obstruction in the Crouch is a 'horse' in the middle of the river, just below Burnham. It is said to dry out at very low water springs. It may be so, but I think there is more water than that. Within half an hour of low water springs I once went aground upon it, drawing five feet six; the mishap seemed to cause surprise, not only to myself but also to knowledgeable locals. It seems impossible to anchor off Burnham, that 'Mecca'—yes, sooner or later the word must be used

47

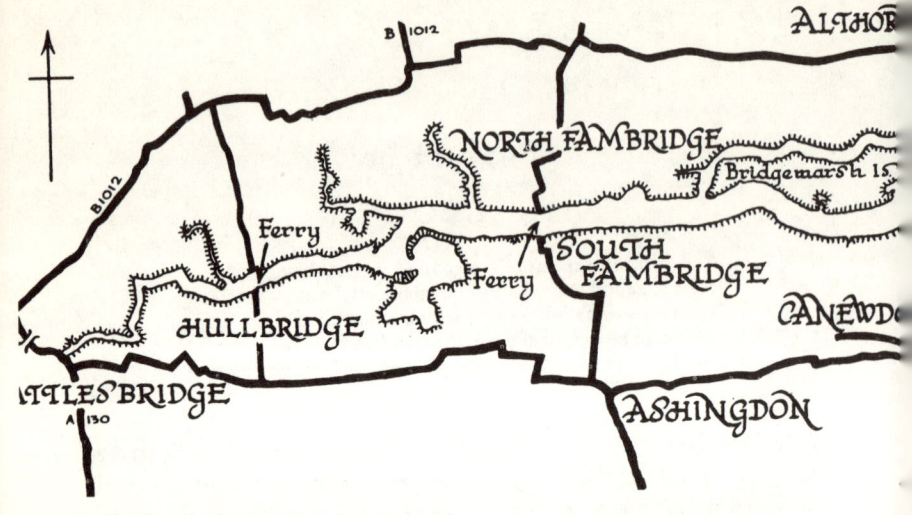

and I might as well say it now and get it over and done with—that 'Mecca' of East Coast yachtsmen.

Hundreds of yachts of all sizes take complete charge of the waters off the front and it would be foolhardy to attempt to bring up a vessel of any size among them. One must anchor above or below. Coming in from sea it is no exaggeration to say that one appears to be approaching a copse in winter-time, so thickly are the masts clustered. Burnham is by far the largest yachting centre on the East Coast, and week-ends in the summer are given over almost entirely to racing.

This form of enjoyment culminates in a perfect orgy of swiftness lasting a whole week at the latter part of the season. What with the rapid gunfire ashore and the falling masts of contenders afloat the affair resembles an old-time naval engagement. During regatta week the river is almost impassable to humble cruisers; one has constantly to jibe, tack or even wear, to avoid the onrush of racers coming from all directions.

Seen from the river, the older parts of the town make as attractive a

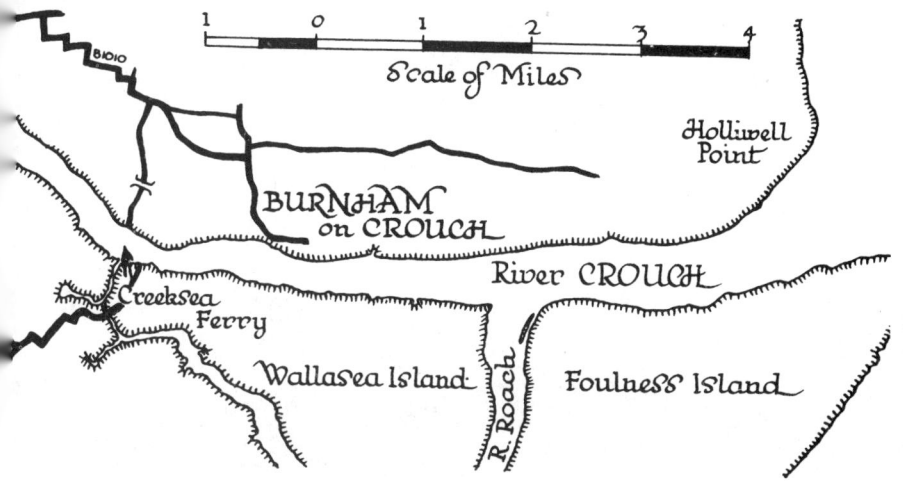

Scale of Miles

waterfront as there is on the East Coast. To see the yachts bobbing about on the fast-moving tide having as a background the mellowed Georgian red-bricked houses standing on the quay is a pleasure.

I once asked a Burnham professional yacht-hand if it were true, as I had heard, that local men were born with webbed feet. He pondered for some time. Then, with ferocity, he shouted, 'It's a damned lie—and I should like to know who fust put it about'.

A little farther up-river and to port is Creeksea. Here also is a considerable yacht anchorage, very likely on account of the clean landing there and the near vicinity of an inn—two excellent reasons. There is also a ferry. Legend has it that a witch, set afloat in a little boat, was drowned here. I don't wonder at it if the trial took place at spring tides with a hard wind. The stream sluices round this Creeksea bend at a 'rate o' knots' and anyone not used to handling a dinghy may easily come to grief.

So far the river banks have been without interest but now the flat country turns to gently rolling slopes running down to the marshes.

On the north side just above Creeksea there is even a cliff. It has been said that here is the very spot upon which Canute sat when he forbade the tide to rise. Bosham in Sussex is also mentioned, among scores of other places, as the scene of the miscalculation.

Canute was certainly at Bosham and his little daughter is reputed to be buried there. In 1865 a great slab of stone was found under the then level of the church, covering a small stone coffin. In the presence of the vicar and four others the seven-inch thick coffin lid was raised, disclosing the remains of a small child.

Farther up-river on the two hills on the southern bank stand the ancient churches of Canewdon and Ashingdon, the scene of a great battle which for a time settled the fate of England.

When the Romans withdrew the British settled down, as they thought, to a tolerable peace. They were not long so to remain for soon the Vikings came to torment them.

The Vikings, though ferocious fighters, were vain. They combed their long fair hair, they trimmed their fierce-looking moustaches and waving beards. They bathed often. Amulets of gold encircled their forearms, coloured beads adorned their necks. The great fur coats worn over their shoulders were held by intricately fashioned brooches of silver and bronze. Their tunics were of dyed wools and coloured linens.

Apart from being the finest seamen of their day they were, above all, fighters. Giving no quarter they expected none. They knew no fear of pain, and death held for them no terrors. For would they not, if they died in battle, be assured of a future life and reside with Thor and Odin in the very heavens themselves?

If a chieftain fell in battle his body would, if at all possible, be put aboard a 'long-ship' and cast adrift on the outgoing tide. The old sages tell us how the craft would be set on fire. As the evening deepened into night the blazing pyre, growing dimmer and yet more dim as it floated away, sank at last, bearing with it the body of the chieftain into that sea of which he had been master. In the gathering darkness straining eyes saw the last flickering flame fly upwards and go out, carrying with it the Soul to take its rightful place among the gods.

Brave the Vikings may have been, cruel they were. They killed for the sake of killing and after a battle put women and children to death for amusement.

In their northern land the winter was spent in rough timbered houses covered with clay and branches of fir. The building would be a single room with curtains hanging a little way from the sides to give some little privacy. In the centre a fire burned on the earthen floor. Food was badly cooked and there were no table manners. The short days and long nights made them glad when the sun began to climb and the spring to come. The time had arrived to prepare their long-ships for sea.

These famous vessels were sometimes as much as a hundred feet long, having a beam of about eighteen feet, and drawing but a few inches of water. The shallow draught made it easy for the crews to

roll the vessels ashore on logs, handy also when it came to passing over the shoals in the estuary of the Thames. Sailing to windward was unknown and the idea of a deep keel to grip the water had not been thought of. A large square sail for running before the wind was hoisted on a shortish mast, sweeps were carried to provide work for the slaves who rowed the craft in the proper direction in a calm. As the new year advanced fitting-out gained pace. New weapons were forged, old ones looked at, their edges made keen at the grindstones. The forge, spare ropes and anchors, canvas and provisions were put aboard; the hundred and one items necessary to support a large number of men for weeks, perhaps months, were stowed away. At last the day came to steer from the fiords for the west and south, bent upon plunder.

With a fair wind the square sail, sometimes with alternate red and white cloths, was hauled to the masthead and the fierce eye of the dragon at the bow pointed in the right direction. In a calm or with a foul wind the sweeps were shipped and, settling into a long, steady swing suitable to the great length of the ship, she forged ahead towards her objective. Days and nights went by. Before the wind fast passages were no doubt made, but many a ship never completed her intended journey. Through force of circumstances or some mismanagement,

the long, shallow craft, getting broadside-on to the steep short seas would be overwhelmed and quickly sink.

As those of them who made the voyage neared the shore the pilot took charge—a man of experience—one who had 'been there before'. Standing and clinging to the figurehead in the bows he would give orders, directing the steersman. His was the eye to first see the waters tumbling and breaking over the shallows guarding the Essex shore. In the darkness his was the ear to catch the noise of the turmoil of the sea. The sail would be hastily lowered and the ship, now under oars, would feel her way in, or anchor.

After so many days at sea the pilot, experienced though he might be, would hardly know exactly to which shoal he had come in the night. But he would know that the sands spread out from the shore like the fingers of a hand and soon, by constantly sounding with the lead, he would be creeping along the lee of a sand. At anchor he could find out the state of the tide. With that knowledge, by pressing on at once or delaying sailing for a time, he would enter a river on the flood. With the coming of the morning the land would be seen. Perhaps the first sight of it showed the red cliffs of Bawdsey, with the town of Ipswich standing at the head of the next river. Or a flood tide at the end of his voyage may have taken him south a bit, so that he saw the Foreland

and the hills of Kent, or the church of St. Peter at Ithancester (which we now call Bradwell) might have been his first landmark. Then, with an easterly breeze and a flowing tide the sail would be hoisted again for a smart run into the Crouch.

The brightly painted shields deco‐ rated with devices in gold and red and blue would be hung over the ship's sides, giving her a more war‐like appearance. The weapons which had been laid aside were wiped of their saltness and taken to the grindstone for a final sharpening.

Helmets reflected the rays of the sun, their eagles' wings nicely adjusted.

The corselet, the only armour they wore apart from the helmet, was put on, the leather straps tightened here and there, the warrior made comfortable and ready for the fray.

Coming fast up-river her crew shouted and sang, as they sought a suitable landing-place. Such being found, the long-ship was set ashore. Almost before her keel found the land the ferocious pirates flung themselves over the sides into the water eager to begin the bloody work of conquering the district. As their feet touched bottom the former sailors became soldiers. Not the well-trained, disciplined troops

such as the Romans before them, but a savage relentless mob. Unlike the Romans, who proceeded methodically to build roads and saw to it that their rear was as strong as their front, the Vikings troubled little about bases, except for the winter.

A solitary long-ship might land its crew. If that crew were defeated there was an end to the matter; if they met with success, often they penetrated too far inland, to be cut off and destroyed before they could regain their boats. But sometimes a number of vessels would come over at the same time, like a little armada. The considerable force thus accumulated would press inland, possessing itself of a fair tract of country wherein to settle during the winter.

Hard on the heels of the Vikings came Angles, Saxons, Jutes and Danes. The Angles and Saxons, were more peace-loving; they settled down to get a living out of the land. The Danes never settled. Like the Vikings, all they wanted was plunder. So long as they could by force of arms inflict fines and ransoms in money or goods, so long did they remain. Like the Vikings they knew no mercy, like the Norsemen they expected none. They had ravaged the northern, eastern and southern parts of England for two or three hundred years. At last it had come to what an American might call 'a show-down'.

In 1016, upon the hill at Canewdon rested the Danes under their chief, Canute. Upon the other hill at Ashingdon lay the Saxons under Edmund Ironside.

The battle might have been won by the Saxons had not Ealdorman Cerdic and his considerable following either run or transferred their allegiance to the Danes. As it was the Saxons were defeated, many of their leaders being slain.

> And all the field beneath
> Shows with a bright variety of death.

By his victory Canute became master of England and so remained for eighteen years.

The church at Canewdon is mainly Perpendicular, finely proportioned with immense buttresses supporting the tower. The hill upon which it stands is scarred still with entrenchments which the learned say are of Danish origin, if not earlier. Here in the seventeenth century there was a quarrel concerning tithes and an entry in the Church Register says something nasty about one of the deceased participants:

CANEWDON CHURCH

Lord, how he swells, as if he had at least
A Commonwealth reposing in his breast.
Prodigious Stomach! Ah, cruelle deale
He could devour whole Churches at a meale.
'Tis very strange that Nature should deliver
So good a stomach to so bad a liver!

The name Canewdon has naturally been associated with Canute, but that invaluable book *The Place-Names of Essex* tells us it simply means 'the hill of Canas's people', older by far than Canute.

Within sight of it, and only three miles away, stands the church of Ashingdon, the 'Assundune' of the Danes. Like that at Canewdon it is surrounded by elms, and the hill upon which it stands also shows very considerable traces of entrenchments made by warriors long ago. Here then, is the very hill upon which Edmund Ironside made his last stand and down which, as an old writer has it 'he swept like lightning'.

Four years after the battle Canute caused a church to be erected to celebrate his victory and there it stands to-day. Altered and built upon of course it is, but with all its restorations it still retains pre-Norman work.

At first sight it seems strange that such a cruel and barbarous people should set up a church. But they had been coming over for several hundreds of years and had, in spite of their nature, assimilated much from the Saxons. Long before, churches had been built in many parts of England and a number of missionaries had for years been preaching Christianity to the people. It is hard to realize that had Canute, who died in 1034, spoken of the Romans (as well he might since there was much of that civilization to be seen), he would be going back six hundred years. It is as though we to-day discussed the battle of Crécy. Such a recession into the past would take us back to Dan Chaucer, before the Peasants' Revolt under Wat Tyler.

Looking down from the hill to the north we see the Crouch winding its silver way before the gently rising grounds on the other side. The sun playing upon the fields brings forward a patch of newly turned earth to let it recede as a cloud sails by. The vivid yellow of a mustard field makes itself seen, to be left by the eye catching the still higher-toned white sails of a yacht heeling to a breeze that ruffles the surface of the river. Below, and come upon by a little lane, nestles South Fambridge, where the inn used to be kept by a character called the 'Alderman'. The inn certainly didn't keep him. Before taking the 'Anchor' he was a coachman—a real old Dickensian coachman, or rather a Shake-spearian coachman, since he was fond of, and ever ready to quote— yes—let's call him once again—'the Swan of Avon'. All round the walls of the rooms of the 'Anchor' hung bugles, whips and pieces of harness; all the paraphernalia of bygone coaching days. He was called 'Alderman' simply because he called everyone else 'Alderman'.

A lively account of him is given in Dr. Halliday Sutherland's *A Time to Keep*—a very fine book.

Here one may cross the river in a dinghy, but to get to North

BATTLESBRIDGE

Fambridge with anything larger than a bicycle it is necessary to go farther up to Battlesbridge. The name which has nothing to do with the battle lately spoken of, is most probably derived from a Saxon named Bataïlle, who owned land hereabouts.

Here the river ceases to be tidal. The little place is picturesque, especially (as all places are) in the evenings, when the great modern mill and the remains of an older one rise up in the gathering darkness like medieval castles.

There is a quay and an inn, called the 'Barge' appropriately enough, since 'spritties' come to the mill. The river dries out soon after half ebb, but seven or eight feet may be found at High Water Springs.

A few yachts have their winter quarters here, but there are (apart from the 'Barge') no facilities for yachting.

Crossing the bridge and making our way down-river we come to North Fambridge, a larger yachting centre than Battlesbridge. Moreover, it boasts a crane on the end of a jetty, very handy for lifting or stepping masts.

Here is another of those out of the way places where everyone does his own work. As at Paglesham, there is one man, Mr. Flick, who looks after the wants of poor yachtsmen and who also works. In the summer-time a nice collection of small yachts rides in the anchorage. The tide runs pretty strongly, which means that being so far up-river, a foul wind rather restricts one's cruising.

My cousin is fond of telling a tale of a Cockney adventuring on the water for the first time. It happened on the Crouch. 'Goin' dahn we kep' goin' from side t'side, not strite dahn mind y', like what you'd fink. The sile kep' swingin' over, 'itting my 'ead. Blawsted nuisance it was! Arter a lot o' this they turned 'er rahnd and let the siles aht proper. Blimey, we didn't 'arf go comin' back!' Not much romance there. Not so romantic as that tale of how a Captain Cammock paid court to the daughter of the then Earl of Warwick, a state of affairs not to the Earl's liking. The lovers were a determined couple, however, and we find them one dark and stormy night at Fambridge in a hurry to cross the river; they had eloped. The ferry-boat, of course, was on the other side (as it always is). What with the howling of the wind and the noise of the waters, shouting brought no response (any more than it does to-day). The captain, suspecting pursuit, decided to swim over and fetch the dinghy. But the lady would have none of it; with him she had come and with him she would go. The pair on horseback therefore plunged into the raging stream. Half-way across they heard their pursuers, one of whose horses neighed. Love pulled the other way. The animal in the river turned round, and in spite of the frantic efforts of the soldier and his love, scrambled back to the bank.

Was the captain run through the body? Was the lady sent away to some solitary tower, there to languish and die? Not a bit of it. You will be glad to know that the party returned to Maldon, from whence they had come. Here, the old Earl, hearing a description of the exploit, relented, since his daughter had, as he said 'ventured her life for his—God bless 'em'. Thereupon, as an old account says, 'they were wedded and bedded!' And to some purpose! The marriage turned out a huge success and abundantly fruitful, as we shall see in another chapter.

An interesting, and earlier, local character was Dr. Bates, who succeeded to his father's living at North Fambridge. He has been described as being 'as magnificent a specimen of a man perhaps, as ever walked arm in arm with fashionable beauty in the groves of Vauxhall'. He was, if ever there was one, a 'man-about-town'. Women, wine, and song were the order of the day and night, and he was constantly in and out of trouble.

Seeing Bates walking quietly in those 'groves of Vauxhall', a party of rowdies headed by Fitzgerald, a notorious brawler of his time, took it into their heads to make trouble. Since the disagreement could not very well be settled in the presence of a lady, a further meeting was arranged in a tavern. There Bates soon found himself in conflict with a 'Captain Miles', really a professional pugilist brought along by Fitzgerald to lend force to the argument. Words gave way to blows; so did 'Captain Miles', who was soundly thrashed by the reverend gentleman.

Not only did Bates partake of the gaieties of the town, but he contributed to them in no small measure by writing and producing plays. Moreover, as editor of the *Morning Post*, he attacked all who gave him offence, and they were many. After falling out with his proprietors he brought out the rival *Morning Herald* in which he continued his onslaughts with renewed vigour to find himself landed in jail on account of a particularly scurrilous libel on the Duke of Richmond. Was Bates 'downed'? Not a bit of it! His ladies and cronies were entertained daily, nightly, and lavishly, in private rooms in the prison from which he emerged with increased popularity.

In the country, as a magistrate, he was the terror of poachers, which recalls the tale of a poacher brought before a magistrate who, if not Bates, may well have been. On being sentenced to twenty years' imprisonment the ancient miscreant burst into tears. 'Oh! My Lord! My Lord!! Consider my age. I cannot possibly complete

the sentence.' 'Never mind,' said the judge kindly, 'do as much of it as you can.'

In spite of his many and bitter conflicts with the Church and in spite of the severity of the criticisms he made of his 'betters', nevertheless this remarkable character had a baronetcy conferred upon him thirteen years before his death, which, if you must know, occurred in 1824.

Fambridge is a nice 'matey' place where everyone helps everyone else and thereby help themselves. In the winter an enthusiastic band of yachtsmen, laden with tools and food, tramps down the lane from the station and disappears into vessels laid up in mud berths. Soon sparks fly up from numerous stove-pipes. Fires have been lit; soon all will be snug and cosy below.

Saturday evenings are merry at the 'Ferry Boat' where the dart is thrown until the hour strikes when the darters themselves are thrown— out. On Sunday mornings, latish, hatches are pushed back and the hermetically sealed yachts emit clouds of foul air. Heads bob up. 'Going ashore?' 'Yes! Half a minute.' The keen week-enders, called again to the bar, consider the programme of work for next week-end. For, by the time the discussion is over, lunch has to be prepared and

63

NORTH FAMBRIDGE

eaten. This necessitates a siesta with cups of tea to follow. There is tidying up to be done, the packing of bags, the almighty rush for that last train. No time to do anything now. But next week end . . .

So the winter passes in pleasurable idleness until one day the sun shines and all is haste and scurry. Those things in the yacht's interior which have been left undone are left undone. Scraping, painting, and varnishing now claim urgent attention. Willing hands withdraw the vessels from their winter quarters, setting them afloat once more.

Flags are mast headed triumphantly. A new season has begun, the best season within living memory!

It is at such places as Fambridge, where they work with their hands, that full enjoyment is experienced. Such as they work for the love of it. When one does that it becomes a pleasure; and one is on the high road to happiness.

CHAPTER IV

STOCK AND DANBURY

Old wooden Knights with legges crossed,
At Danbury quiet lie.
How brave they look in mail imbossed,
How sad that they should die.
JANE LE FINCH

SOONER or later when you come to explore the rivers of Essex and Suffolk you will travel along the main Colchester–Ipswich road. Branch off at Ingatestone for Stock. A little way along the road, turn round and spare a minute to look at Ingatestone church tower. A fine thing to see. Lofty, with parapets and battlements, its lovely red brickwork cross-diapered with black has such a rich mellowness, that in the sunshine of a setting sun it seems to be almost on fire with light.

The road winds through country where a good deal of hunting goes on. I can see no justification for fox-hunting by present methods, but the sight of a 'hunt' on a fine sparkling November morning certainly gladdens the eye, if not the heart.

Very likely the colour of the huntsmen's coats stimulates the mind and gives a brave appearance. It was partly for this reason that soldiers wore red tunics. It aided recruiting (and attracted nursemaids). It served also to minimize the appearance of blood when a warrior was wounded.

Approaching Stock, the first thing you see is the church, set picturesquely on a small hill. It is one of those little churches with a wooden tower and belfry. About five hundred years ago there was a sudden demand for belfries. The Greenwich time-signal had not been thought of; the majority of people took their time from the sun. The arrival at church, therefore, had none of that nice precision attained

65

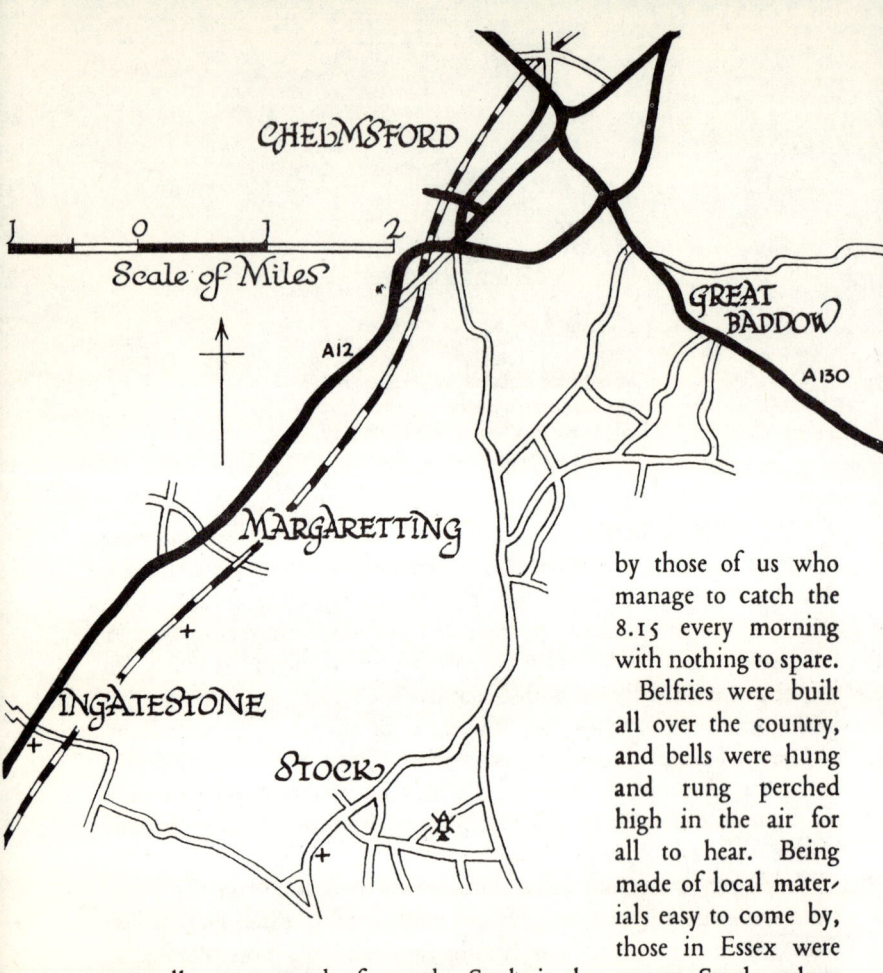

Scale of Miles

by those of us who
manage to catch the
8.15 every morning
with nothing to spare.

Belfries were built
all over the country,
and bells were hung
and rung perched
high in the air for
all to hear. Being
made of local mater-
ials easy to come by,
those in Essex were
generally constructed of wood. Such is the case at Stock, where
the belfry and tower were clapped on to the west wall of the church
—and a very pretty job they made of it.

Some time ago I caused a yacht to be built. Controversy arose over
it size and shape; former friends became almost enemies. There was a
difference of opinion over its rig. Some said the internal arrangements
were the best they had ever seen (Yes! They were invited to the launch
and the subsequent 'high jinks'.) Others said they were the worst.

66

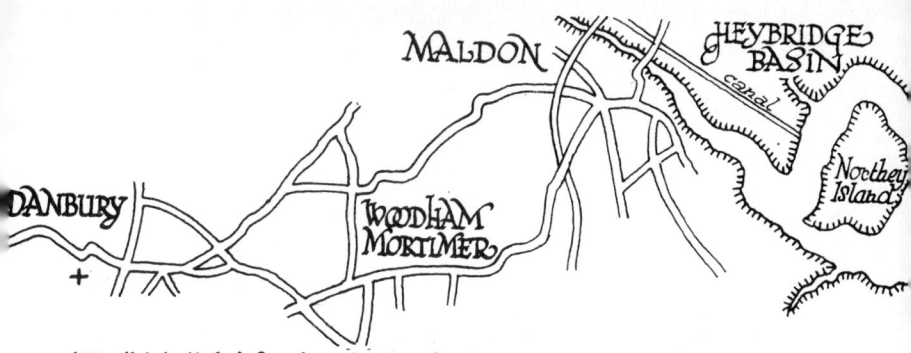

(No 'high jinks' for them.) But the fiercest arguments of all concentrated upon the *way* she was built. Some said the frames should be thin and steam-bent. Then, they said, the vessel would 'give' as she moved through the water.

The other school of thought advocated large heavy frames and plenty of 'em. Each was to have its natural curve. Then the yacht would be as solid and 'ungiving' as it was possible to make it.

It was surprising to find such an exact opposition of thought; surprising, too, was the ferocity with which the two schools contended. One builder held it a wicked thing to even think of constructing a boat other than with the very heaviest of materials. 'Look at him,' he said, referring to a rival craftsman—'builds boats with steamed frames— and him a Methodist.' I was shown hulls which I thought at the time were massively constructed. I hadn't seen the inside of the belfry at Stock. Those vessels, of whose great strength and weight their owners boasted, were it possible to have brought them to Stock, would have looked like wicker-baskets alongside the belfry. I tell you, it is worth looking at.

Inside the church itself is a brass effigy to Richard Twedye Esquire, who, as is recorded on his monument,

> Four alms-houses here hath he bilte,
> For four poor nights to dwell,
> And them indowed with stypends large
> Enough to keep them well.

The 'stypend' was twelve pence a week with eight shillings a year for 'livery'. But then money went farther in those days.

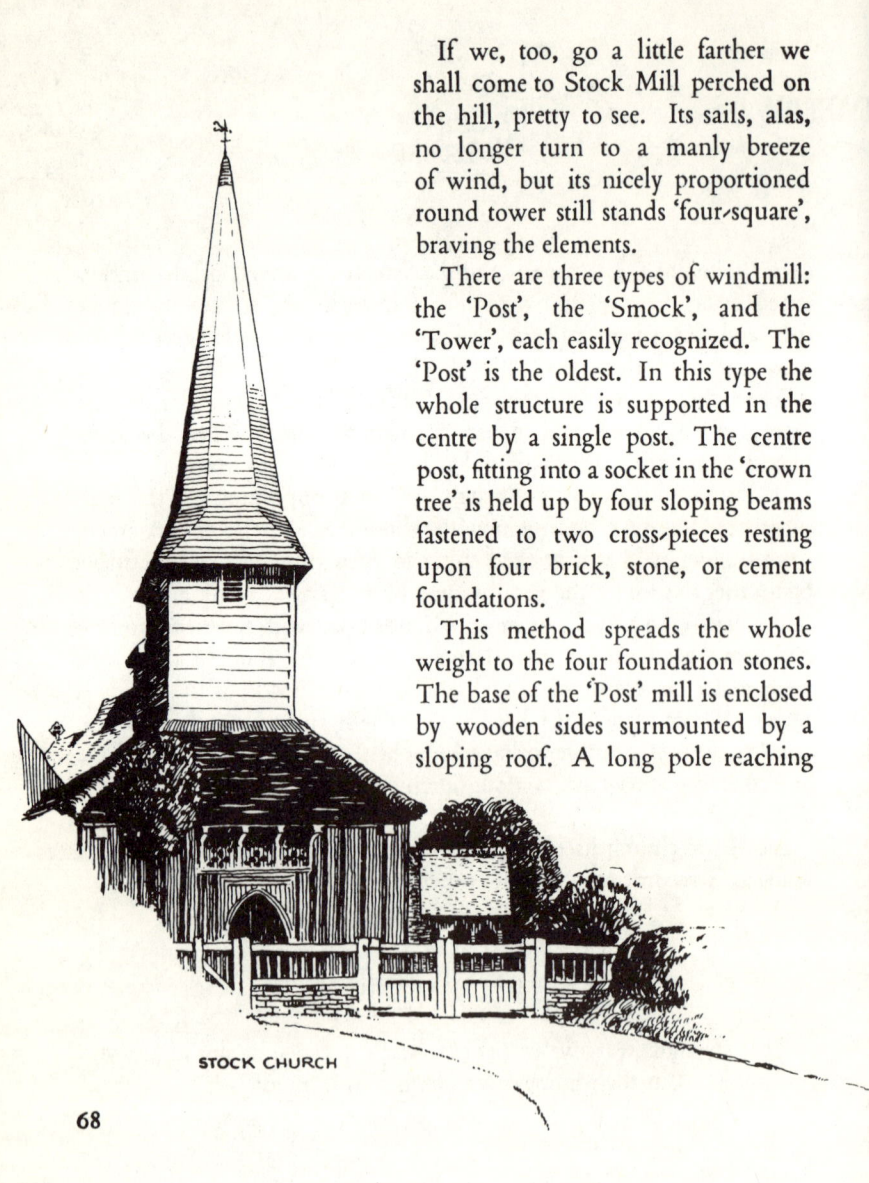

STOCK CHURCH

If we, too, go a little farther we shall come to Stock Mill perched on the hill, pretty to see. Its sails, alas, no longer turn to a manly breeze of wind, but its nicely proportioned round tower still stands 'four-square', braving the elements.

There are three types of windmill: the 'Post', the 'Smock', and the 'Tower', each easily recognized. The 'Post' is the oldest. In this type the whole structure is supported in the centre by a single post. The centre post, fitting into a socket in the 'crown tree' is held up by four sloping beams fastened to two cross-pieces resting upon four brick, stone, or cement foundations.

This method spreads the whole weight to the four foundation stones. The base of the 'Post' mill is enclosed by wooden sides surmounted by a sloping roof. A long pole reaching

STOCK CHURCH BELFRY

69

'POST' MILL

from the top almost to the ground was used to swing the entire mill round bodily. It was possible for a strong man to turn it to the wind, but more often a horse was used.

'Post' mills lasted several hundreds of years, but in the sixteenth century a new idea was conceived, the cap only, and not the entire mill, being turned. They came to be known as 'Smock' or 'Tower'

'SMOCK' MILL

mills. The 'cap', running on rollers, carried the wind-shaft, to which the sails were secured, together with the various machinery for the gearing of them. It too had a long pole to the ground by which the sails were turned to the wind; the method is used in Holland to-day.

In 1750, however, a Scotsman named Andrew Meikle invented a sort of rudder, which kept the sails to the wind automatically. It consisted of a six- to ten-bladed fan set on the opposite side of the cap to the sails and at right-angles to them. The wind, changing direction, turned the fan, which by an arrangement of gears on a rack, brought the sails into position again.

This movable cap type took, as I say, two forms—the 'Tower' and the 'Smock'. The 'Tower', as at Stock, is usually of brick, covered sometimes with plaster, tapering towards the top on which the cap revolves. The 'Smock' is more often than not octagonal and built of wood. One of its characteristics is the very large platform all round, handy when the sails need attention. The type is so called because it

71

TOWER MILL

resembles somewhat the old-fashioned smock which, alas, countrymen no longer wear.

It can do no harm to try, with the help of a diagram, to explain briefly how a mill works. The sails are fixed to, and turn, the 'wind-shaft'. At the inner end of the 'wind-shaft' inside the mill the great toothed brake-wheel engages the much smaller horizontal 'wallower'.

The 'wallower' surmounts the centre-post going down through the various floors. On each floor more cogwheels engage the grindstones. Now then! The wind blows the sails round, turns the 'wind-shaft' and brake-wheel, and so the 'wallower'. If the 'wallower' turns so must the centre-post. To make the stones revolve the miller engages the cogwheels on the various floors, and the trick is done. Each pair of stones can be thrown out of gear independently should there not be sufficient work for them all.

In spite of this brief account the diagram, though not to scale, shows clearly why, when the sails go round, the mill-stones go round too.

Yes, but how is the grain actually ground? Well, like everything

72

else it is simple when you know how. Each mill-stone measures about four feet across and both are scored, one right-handed, the other left-handed, with a series of grooves. The angle these grooves take from the centre is most important; if it is not absolutely right the mill won't grind. (I was looking at the inside of a coffee-grinder the other day and, although tapered, the pattern on the grinders was a replica of the grooves in a mill-stone.)

The stones are cunningly ground. At the centre, called the 'eye', the width between them is such that a piece of brown paper can be nicely gripped. In the middle, the 'breast', it is possible to insert a

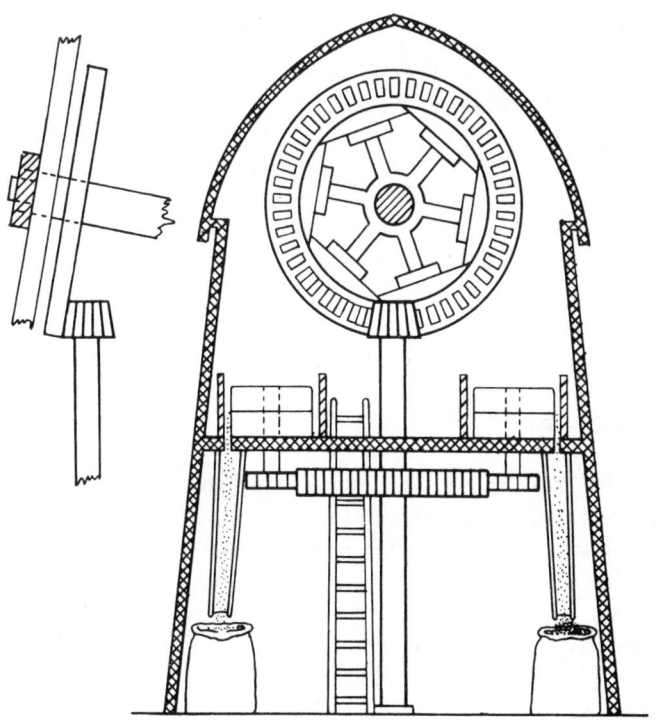

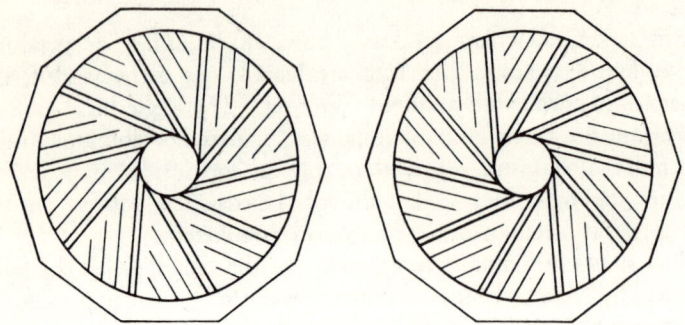

piece of newspaper. At the outer edge, or 'skirt', the width is just enough to take a piece of tissue paper. The adjustment is as nice as that. The lower, or 'bed' stone, never moves. In a hole in its centre a spindle is tapered at the top into an oblong piece called the 'mace', having an arm let into it. Upon this arm, which is cemented to the upper stone, an iron contrivance called 'the damsel' is fixed. All this gear, enclosed by a cylinder let tightly into the upper stone, revolves with it.

The grain poured into the hopper falls into a trough called a 'shoe'. According to what is to be ground so the 'shoe' is adjusted, but the angle is never so steep that the grain flows down of its own accord. The lower end of the tapered 'shoe' is cut away to make room for 'the damsel'.

We have seen how the sails turn the centre-post and so, through the cogged wheels, revolve the spindle passing through the bed-stone. Since 'the damsel' is fixed to it she, too, goes round, her four rods striking the sides of the shoe in so doing.

The grain, knocked down the gentle slope, passes 'the damsel' into the cylinder, and comes eventually to the centre of the top of the bed-stone. The weight of further grain compels it to enter the space between the two stones. Round and round and out and out it goes, getting finer and finer, to fall at last from the outer edge in the form of flour. The stones are enclosed by wooden cases which control the

74

flour until it finds its way to a hole in the floor through which it falls down a shute into waiting sacks. Again, I say, in spite of this account the diagram shows how the miller works the oracle.

The first mention of windmills in England is to be found in the Chronicles of Joscelyn de Brakelonde of Bury St. Edmunds. Readers of (and I hope there still *are* readers of) Carlyle's *Past and Present* will remember Abbot Samson's 'terrible flash of anger' when poor old Herbert, the Dean, erected a windmill for his own use. Such was Samson's rage that he sent his carpenters to pull it to pieces.

Old Herbert, tottering as fast as his failing legs could carry him, protested to the Abbot that the wind was free, and no man could deny him the benefit of it. 'I am as obliged to thee as if thou hadst cut off both my feet,' roared Samson. 'By God's face I will not eat bread until

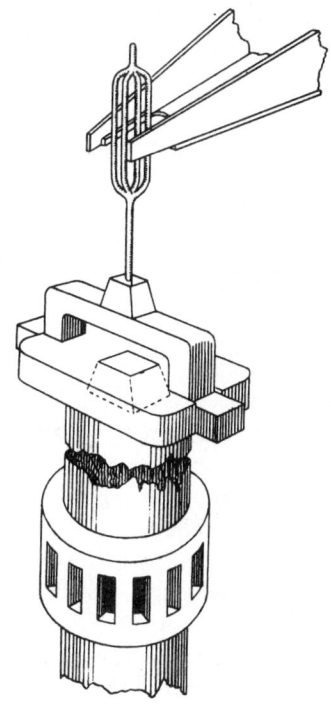

that fabric be torn to pieces—I tell thee that it will not be without damage to my mills; for the townsfolk will go to thy mill and grind their corn at their own good pleasure, nor can I hinder them since they are free men.' All Herbert's powers of persuasion were of no avail against such a temper supported by self-interest, and his 'fabric' was pulled down.

We see in the passage quoted, evidence of the power of the miller and how jealous he was of his rights. In those olden days each manor had either a water-mill or a windmill, and the people of that manor were compelled to send their corn to it to be ground. The miller kept a certain portion of flour as reward for his service. He tended to grind the poor as well as their grain, since he had a monopoly. He put aside more and more for himself until Acts of Parliament were passed, compelling him to act more justly. He was restrained, for obvious reasons, from keeping chickens and hogs, nor was he allowed to water the corn; it weighed more that way.

The rollicking 'I care for nobody, no, not I, and nobody cares for me!' had the elements of truth. It is not true to-day. All the millers I have met have been jolly, or at least as jolly as the income-tax authorities allow. If you ask them nicely they will generally let you look over their 'fabric' and perhaps tell you its history if they have the time.

The corn which the windmills used to grind is now treated by modern machinery; all that is left to them now is the coarser cereals. Thus they are falling into disuse and so to decay, and a picturesque feature of the English landscape tends to pass.

It is heartening to know that the Essex County Council have been so far-sighted as to save such mills in the county as are worth saving, and with that aid there are still one or two in Essex which earn, if they do not get, a living by grinding 'grist'.

Various devices enable windmill sails to be reefed like ships and some, as at Stock, have caps fashioned like a great dinghy turned bottom upwards, as though the mill had taken it into her head to have everything snugged down nicely for a voyage across the world. Just as a skipper of one of the old-time grain ships off the Horn would carry all sail until the last possible moment before reefing down in safety, so used the old millers to 'go at it' day and night, vying one with the other in sail-carrying, especially if two mills were within sight of each other. They knew as much about the weather as any seaman ever did.

A miller told me that often when he was fast asleep in bed the slightest change in direction or force of the wind would become known to him; out he would spring at once to see that the hoppers were being properly fed, lest by running hot the stones shot sparks on to the bone-dry floors and set the mill on fire.

It was day and night work in the busy season after harvest, interspersed perhaps with calm, quiet, idle days in September.

Those were the days when gleaners went into the fields to pick up wheat. But not until the 'policeman' had gone.

The 'policeman' was a 'stook' of corn left in the middle of the field when the last hay-wain had left. It was well worth the farmer's while to rake up the leavings of the reaper and binder, and not until this was done and the 'policeman' taken away was gleaning allowed. Then into the fields we used to go, children and women, with now and then an old, old man. What we gathered was sent to be ground, the miller keeping some for himself perhaps, or receiving hard cash.

The sacks of flour, kept in a dry place, lasted well into the winter, and the home-made bread and cakes we ate were fit for the King of England.

As you leave Stock on the way to Maldon, Danbury Hill looms up on the far horizon. To Essex eyes it looks very like a mountain. Reaching a height of but 300 feet the level country gives it an air almost of grandeur.

The Danes (hence Danbury) knew how to pick a site for defence; they were pretty safe here from a surprise attack, perched as they were on the eminence. Now at the very top stand the 'Griffin' and Danbury church. With its fine stone tower and tall spire, the church, a landmark for miles round, contains much of interest. It contains, not one, but two, 'squints'; one in the priests' room to the north of the chancel, the other piercing the wall of the north aisle.

Squints? What are 'squints' and what are they for? 'Well,' as we say in Essex, 'we don't rightly know.' No one rightly knows. Like the Dene Holes they are an unsolved mystery. They are quite common, but two in one church, as here, is unusual.

Squints are narrow slits cut either through the outside walls of a church or through a wall or column within. They are generally

77

between five and six feet above the ground, and in every case the altar is to be seen through them. That is about all that anyone knows. Several theories have been put forward to account for them, but they never quite explain everything.

One reason given is that the priest, at the moment prior to the Elevation of the Host, could ring a bell for those outside to hear. Apart from there being no particular reason why he should do so at all, it would be very difficult for him to thrust his arm (and it would have to be an arm almost as long as the law's) through a squint, especially holding a tiny bell. Far better to attract attention by going to the open door to give a hearty peal on some hand-bells. Nor does the theory explain interior squints.

Another name for squints is 'leper holes'. Cut off from the world by the nature of their contagious disease lepers were not allowed inside a church. It has been suggested that the slits in the outside walls were made to allow these poor unfortunate people to witness the Elevation of the Host from outside. A nice thought, but again facts override theory. Squints are so narrow that one has literally to squint through them—hence the name.

It would be difficult for more than one person at a time to view the interior unless they stood in line, one behind the other, the short in front, the tall behind. It would have been very easy to have made large windows rather than bore through the sometimes immense thickness of a wall. Nor again, does the theory account for interior squints.

We are sure of the habits of people who lived thousands of years before Christ was born, what they did, and their reasons for doing so. It is, then, the more extraordinary that these strange architectural features should have crept into churches so well within recorded history, yet we know nothing of their origin or purpose.

The most interesting features of the church, however, are the three effigies of knights carved in wood. They are clad in splendid mail armour and lie with their legs crossed. It used to be thought that effigies so postured represented men who had fought in the Crusades, but it is not necessarily so. Two of the Danbury figures are supposed to be members of the St. Clair family; the armour of one shows knee-caps, so proving it to be of a later period than the other. Chain armour used to chafe knees and arms so much that knee-caps and elbow gussets were invented to give additional comfort to the warrior. These thirteenth-century figures are reckoned to be among the best examples of their kind in England.

In 1779, men working in the church discovered a great stone which, when raised, revealed a leaden coffin. Inside, another of elm protected a shell containing a body lying in a liquor or pickle, 'somewhat resembling mushroom catsup'. A workman confirmed its appearance

DANBUR'

by sampling the liquor, which, he said, tasted as much like catsup as it looked—perhaps it *was*!

The body, thought to be that of Sir Gerald Braybrooke, who died in 1422, was re-interred and has since been left to rest in peace.

The church itself has also been disturbed, twice at least by lightning and once by the Devil who 'kicked up a rumpus'. According to Hollingshed: 'Upon Corpus Christy day in the year 1402, the Third of Henry the Fourth; at Evensong time, the Devil entered the Church in the likness of a Gray-frier, and raging horribly, playing his parts like a devil indeed, to the great astonishment and feare of the parish-ioners; and the same houre with a tempest of whorle-wind and thunder, the top of the steeple was broken downe and halfe of the chancel scattered abroad.'

Five hundred years have gone since this startling occurrence, and there is no record of Satan's having appeared in Essex since. He was, according to Belloc, 'last heard of at Brighton', but how recently he does not say.

Across the road from the church the 'Griffin' is a fine Elizabethan inn, with twisted beams and windows overlooking an old-world garden, a really old-world garden, such as one finds only in the heart of the country.

Years ago many of us tried to be soldiers in Danbury Park, a fine spacious, wooded place. From the top of the hill the panorama stretches away beyond Chelmsford as far as eye can carry. From the southern slopes one can look across country over the Thames and on a clear day see the hills of Kent. To the eastward, like a silver serpent the great Blackwater river winds its way down to the sea.

Let us wind our way there too, descending from Danbury to the flatlands so characteristic of the Essex seaboard.

CHAPTER V

THE BLACKWATER RIVER:
SOUTH BANK

. . . for gift give spears
The poisoned point, and the old sword.
THE 'SONG OF MALDON'

THERE is no river in the British Isles to compare with the Blackwater. For me the matter is settled beyond question. There are those other rivers of the south: the Dart, the Fal, and that river running past Salcombe. There are those Scottish lochs open to the sea, which may be classed as rivers. All have much to commend them. But to me the Blackwater is their master—it is my home. And upon my soul—and putting aside what looks very much like a prejudice—there is so much about it which is good, that I find no reason to apologize.

Does it not run for some seventeen miles from Maldon to the sea—a distance great enough for any reasonable yachtsman to play in? Its lowlying banks permit the winds of heaven to blow truly and freely across its ample bosom. Its anchorages are many, safe, and quiet; its tides are not immoderate. It has a spaciousness—an air of freedom; a largeness and a character all its own. I love it.

The river is deepest on its southern side, where the tide flows for some twenty minutes after it has turned on the Mersea shore.

Very likely you will see a barge at anchor waiting for the tide to take her into Bradwell, to which we are bound.

The Creek, like a dog's hind leg, has been made more difficult of successful entry than it really is by many yachting writers who have encompassed it about with compass bearings.

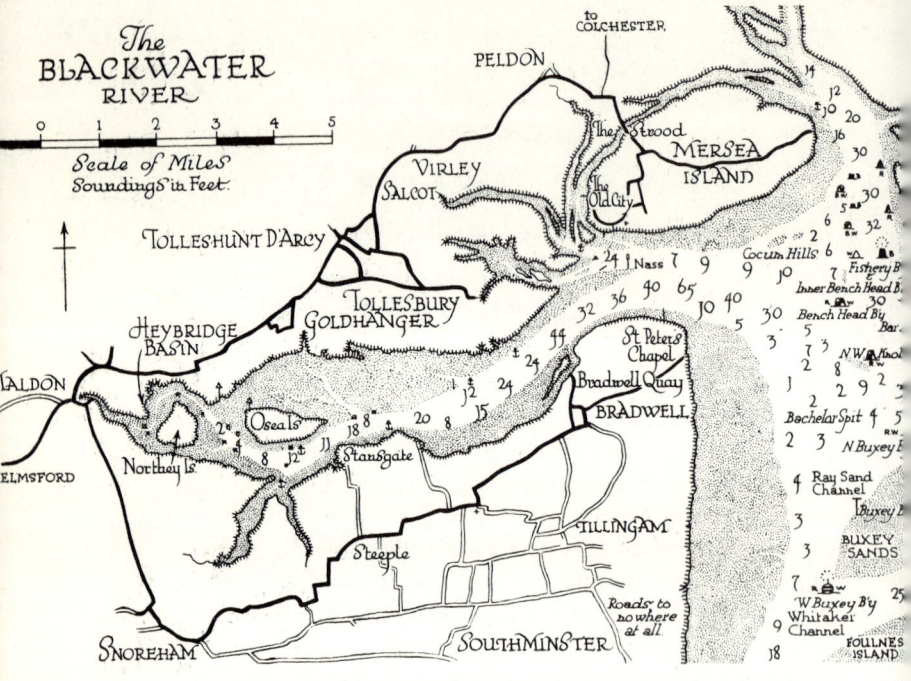

The BLACKWATER RIVER

0 1 2 3 4 5
Scale of Miles
Soundings in Feet

to COLCHESTER

PELDON

VIRLEY
SALCOT

The Strood

The Old City

MERSEA ISLAND

TOLLESHUNT D'ARCY

TOLLESBURY
GOLDHANGER

HEYBRIDGE BASIN

MALDON

CHELMSFORD

Northey Is

Osea Is

Nass

Cocum Hills

Fishery B.
Inner Bench Head B.
Bench Head By.
Bar.

NW Knol

Bachelar Spit

N Buxey B.

Ray Sand Channel

I Buxey B.

BUXEY SANDS

W Buxey By
Whitaker Channel

FOULNES ISLAND

St Peters Chapel

Bradwell Quay

BRADWELL

Stansgate

Steeple

TILLINGAM

Roads to nowhere at all

SNOREHAM

SOUTHMINSTER

Once you recognize that there is more mud than water half the battle of getting into the creek has been won. It should never be fought at all if your boat draws a fathom of water; call it a draw and lie comfortably afloat just at the entrance; the row to the quay gives, if not an appetite, at least a thirst.

A vessel of smaller draught can find her way in, as she can anywhere else, with a chart and lead-line. Keep two beacons on Peewit Island in line. As the creek opens out at right-angles to port, turn with it, keeping over to the starboard side. Gradually cross the channel now, being guided ahead by stakes daubed with white paint. Turn again as near as may be along the line of moored craft and you are safely at the quay. Take no notice whatever of the substantial stakes planted in lines on either side of the channel. They served to guide aircraft during the war and are of no service to yachtsmen. They dry out. Beyond, the creek meanders on, getting increasingly shallow, to merge rather than run into the Blackwater again.

At the quay there is good clean landing at all states of the tide, and one soon discovers the 'Green Man'. Many yachtsmen discover it immediately on rounding the bend in the creek, for it stands out boldly on

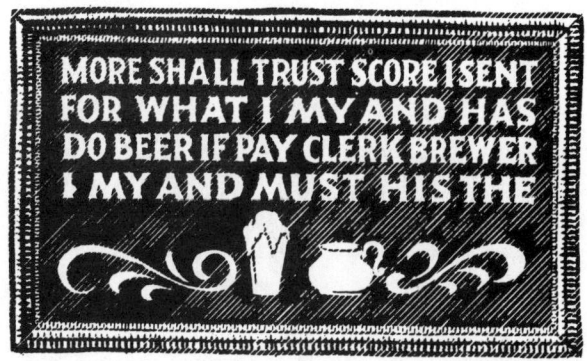

the side of the road with a field before it sloping to the water's edge. These enthusiasts fasten their eyes upon the inn, keeping their bowsprits pointing generally in its direction. Some keep a certain chimney in line with a bush in the foreground. Others make no bones about it, but steer for the open door, running aground before reaching it. By the time they have shoved off or waded ashore precious moments have been lost, and oft-times, as panting and dishevelled figures come hurrying up the road, the door closes, the bolt is shot, and the awful cry goes up, 'Too late! Too late!' They also have shot their bolt.

Of late years the 'Green Man' has been altered considerably, but in the public bar you may still see a good old-fashioned fireplace, over which hangs a curiously worded board. My drawing of it may serve to puzzle the reader for a moment or two, but no prizes are offered for its solution.

THE LITTLE SHOP AT BRADWELL QUAY.

A little farther up the road towards the village is a shop with over-hanging windows, where old-time bull's-eyes may be bought. The door opens in two parts, an upper and lower, like a stable. As you enter, a little bell tinkles. Inside there is the aroma of acid-drops, the sweetness of 'licorice all-sorts'; a whiff of new bread mingling with the odour of carbolic soap.

From behind the counter almost anything may be produced: tallow candles, packets of stomach powders, linen lines, paraffin lamp-wicks, 'sugardecandy'—anything.

Shops such as these are in the nature of an adventure. It is ten chances to one you will come away carrying a mouse-trap or a pair of bicycle clips; but no matter, the experience is worth the price.

By the side of the shop a lane leads past some cottages, whose gardens with their box-hedges and old-fashioned flowers such as the phlox, the sweetly scented moss-rose, and 'pinks' (which are white) are a joy to behold. Bees drone from lily to lily. They amble across to the honeysuckle and, laden with nectar, arrive leisurely at the door of their beehives in the sun, waddle in, and disappear.

In Bradwell village itself there stands proof of the wickedness of Victorian days —the village lock-up.

BRADWELL LOCKUP

As late as 1840 the law required each village to provide temporary accommodation for law-breakers, and lock-ups were the result. There are still quite a few scattered about the country, but it is surprising there are not more, seeing how short a time it is since they were officially discontinued.

The Bradwell lock-up, hard by the church, is so small that there could have been no anticipation of crime breaking out on a grand scale. On each side of the door, which has a grating, are hinged irons, shaped to accommodate the wrists of wastrels. At a 'pinch' (if one may use the expression) father, mother, a son and daughter might all have been held in the grip of the law at the same time. Nearby is another reminder of

STEPS FOR THE GENTRY AT BRADWELL.

bygone days. Built on to the wall against the church gate are stone steps surmounted by an iron post. These enabled the gentry to descend and ascend as they came on horseback to worship.

The road beside which these two relics stand leads past the 'Cricketers' inn. Since we are not cricketing we ought also to pass it, going on through fields to what is perhaps the oldest ecclesiastical building in England: St. Peter-ad-Murum—the Chapel of St. Peter-on-the-Wall. Here the Romans built a considerable fortress called Othona. It occupied an area of about six acres and was garrisoned by five or six hundred soldiers known as the Fortenses—the 'braves'. They were commanded by the 'Count of the Saxon Shore', whose jurisdiction ran as far north as Norfolk. He who bore such a splendid title must have had a wearying time of it looking out across the bleak and cheerless North Sea straining his eyes for a sight of the Norsemen who had begun to threaten the coasts of Britain.

But Rome started to crumble, and the day came when the legions left this bleak outpost and turned for home. Then warriors came from the north bent on plunder, overrunning the land; the country was divided and ruled by several powerful men who called themselves 'kings'.

Sigberd was the powerful man ruling over these parts. Becoming a Christian, he asked his friend, the King of Northumbria, to send someone who would preach and convert his followers. So it came about that Cedde was consecrated Bishop of the East Saxons. Othona, now called Ithancester by the Saxons, was for some obscure reason made the gospel-spreading headquarters. Cedde seems to have chosen the most ungetatable place he could find. Nevertheless, with an abundance of Roman material to hand, the Chapel of St. Peter was built actually in the walls of the former fortress.

This happened round about the year A.D. 654. The buildings were, of course, much larger than the remains we see to-day, consisting as they do of four upstanding well-preserved walls roofed over, ready to last as long, and longer, than they have already.

The chapel was used for many years as a barn, but a generous donor judiciously restored the fabric, and now every year a service is held within its rededicated walls. It is also the object of pilgrimages. I saw one such walking through the fields, headed by priests and acolytes bearing incense, chanting as they went. It required but little imagination to go back thirteen hundred years.

The country round about must have been much the same; a few more trees perhaps. Perhaps not so many. Looking across to Colne Point and East Mersea one saw what Bishop Cedde must have seen. The tide creeps in as it did then. Very likely the chanting of the pilgrims differed but little from those of old, for they were simple, sweet, and fundamental tunes.

As I write I can see the Chapel of St. Peter across the river, catching the last rays of the setting sun. There, perhaps, is the oldest building in England from which Christianity has been preached. One cannot look upon it, if one looks well, without emotion. There comes a deep sense of humility when one tries to realize how long this sentinel has stood at the end of the land, what it has stood for, and what it *will* stand for until the end of time.

At Fambridge we saw what manner of man the Reverend Bates was. Before he went there he held the living at Bradwell and was, no doubt, as great a scourge to poachers hereabouts as he was at Fambridge.

One remembers talk of another scourge, for we are fairly in that part of Essex called the Dengie Hundred, said to be ridden with ague. It all started, at least publicly, with John Norden, who published a description of the county in 1594. 'But I cannot,' he wrote, 'commend the healthfullness of it: and especially nere the sea coastes, Rochford, Denge, Tendering Hundredes, and other lowe places about the creekes which gave me a most cruel quarterne fever.' Happily he added: 'But the maine and sweete comodeties countervayle the daunger.' Damage, however, was done. Between sixty and seventy years later Thomas Fuller in his *Worthies of England* repeated the slander, saying 'the Easting is not very healthful or the Aire thereof'.

Lastly comes Defoe, that great romancer, who began publishing his *Tour Through Great Britain* in 1724. Let him tell his tale. 'I have one remark more, before I leave this damp part of the world, and which I cannot omit on the women's account; namely, that I took notice of a strange decay of the sex here; insomuch, that all along this county it was very frequent to meet with men that had had from five or six to fourteen or fifteen wives; nay, and some more; and I was inform'd that in the marshes on the other side of the river over against Candy Island, there was a farmer, who was then living with the five and twentieth wife, and that his son who was but about thirty-five years old, had already had about fourteen; indeed this part of the story I only had by report, tho' from good hands too; but the other is well known and easie to be inquired in to, about Fobbing, Curringham, Thundersly, Benfleet, Prittlewell, Wakering, Great Stambridge, Cricksea, Burnham Dengy and other towns of the like situation. The reason, as a merry fellow told me, who said he had had about a dozen and half of wives, (tho' I found out afterwards he fibbed a little) was this: That they being bred in the marshes themselves, and season'd to the place, did pretty well with it; but that they always went up into the hilly country, or, to speak their own language, into the uplands for a wife. That when they took the young lasses out of the wholesome and fresh air, they were healthy, fresh and clear and well; but when they came out of their native air into the marshes among the fogs and damps, there they presently chang'd their complexion, got an ague or two, and seldom held it above half a year, or a year at most; and then, said he, we go to the uplands again and fetch another; so that marrying of wives was reckon'd a kind of good farm to them. It is true, the fellow told this

90

in a kind of drollery, and mirth; but the fact, for all that, is certainly true; and that they have abundance of wives by that very means.'

Reading Defoe, one would imagine the inhabitants of the Dengie Hundreds to be like Milton's 'Sheep',

> . . . swoln with wind, and the rank mist they draw,
> Rot inwardly, and foul contagion spread.

If Defoe is to be believed, one thinks of them as a wheezy, decrepit race of people, coughing and trembling, wreathed about in fogs, glad indeed of an occasional shaft of watery sunshine to instil a trace of warmth into their palsied limbs. They were, and are, of course, just like you or me, and the ladies are as buxom and live to as ripe an age in the Dengie Hundreds as anywhere else. Certainly there are fogs in the winter, and in the summer too; these latter usually presage the coming of a fine hot day. The winter fogs, however, are not confined solely to the marshes. They spread inland, enveloping even the great heart of the British Empire itself, polluted, moreover, by the industrialism of that great city and no longer clean as on the coast. There the east wind blows fresh from the sea, and if it 'fare perishes you with the cowd', that same wind 'perishes' the perishers in, say, Maddox Street.

That the marshes may be bleak in the winter I will neither affirm nor deny; I leave that to the late Rider Haggard, whose fine description of them makes one warm one's hands by the fire.

But I will say that the road from Bradwell to Maldon is full of charm, twisting, turning, and winding continually, defeating speed, which is as it should be—there is no need for hurry here. Take it easy and gently, like the country, and have a look round. Turn the car off along any of the roads running down towards the sea. They never reach it,

neither perhaps will you. But it will be an afternoon well spent if you lie in the grass, if you hear the sough of the wind over the marshes, if you hear the lark singing as it hovers over its nest. And if you reach the sea across the fields, then sit and watch the tide seeping in relent/lessly, rising gradually higher and higher, cutting off, surrounding, and making an island of a purple saffron/crowned hump of mud in the channel of a little creek. Foraging its way into nooks and crannies it reaches the roots of the sturdy plants. Higher still, the current now gurgles past the stems, moving them to and fro, shaking them so that they seem to be signalling one to the other. The purple flowers wave a last inevitable farewell as, like the earth in which they grow, they too are engulfed by the tide.

Thinking on these things it is perhaps worth while mentioning the 'bird/tides'. The 'spring' tides of June are naturally lower than other 'springs', and it is said that God in his wisdom has ordered it so for the benefit of sea birds nesting in the marshes, whose little ones would drown if the tides reached the height they at other times attain. A pretty thought.

On the river side of the Dengie Hundred the roads, as to seaward, also come to an end in a field, except at Stone Point in St. Lawrence Bay, a popular week/end resort with a beach sloping steeply, capital for bathing.

A little farther up/river is Stansgate Abbey, an abbey, alas, in name only, except for a small piece of wall now part of farm buildings. Still farther towards the river's source, Lawling Creek, with its offshoot, Mayland Creek, sprawls far inland. At its entrance opposite Osea Island there is but a couple of feet of water at low water springs, but immediately within are depths of two fathoms. A nice anchorage for a summer's night in June, when one sits in the cockpit smoking an after/dinner pipe in the cool of the day watching the yachts drifting up lazily on the last of the flood to Mill Beach.

Across the river on Osea Island a figure comes tramping along the little jetty to light an oil lamp at its extremity. One by one riding lights are hoisted. As the sun dips down behind Maldon, throwing the town into noble purple silhouette, what little wind there was dies away. A glassy calm comes over the river. At the turn of the tide the 'Doctor', that buoy guarding the shoal off Osea, nods his head as he leans in the opposite direction, composing himself for a six-hour sleep. For him the day is done, but for the tide another 'shift' has begun; another life—since it must grow from infancy to manhood, from man-hood to old age, to lose its strength and finally die, to be at that very moment born again destined to visit the scenes of its former existence or live for a little while in new surroundings.

'From the marshes and low grounds, being not able to travel without many windings and indentures, by reason of the creeks, and waters, I came up to the town of Maldon.' So writes our old friend Defoe. So one must go to-day with 'many windings and indentures'.

Defoe comes to grief (not that it would worry him) in associating Maldon with Camulodunum, very likely because he had read Camden who printed the heresy. The Roman colony of Camulodunum occupied the site upon which Colchester now stands, as all the world knows. Beyond referring the reader to Camden for an account of the British rising under Boadicea, Defoe says nothing about the town itself. Yet Maldon (which was known to Ptolemy as Idumania) is interesting. Whether the British queen defeated the ninth and fourteenth legions at Maldon or no will perhaps never be rightly determined. The very learned who forage about to establish the truth of the matter have come to the conclusion that the battle was fought somewhere between the town and Colchester, very likely at Messing.

We are on surer, albeit marshier, ground when we talk of the Battle of Maldon. We know a good deal about this conflict between Saxon and Dane, because one who, even if he himself was not present, knew someone who was, and wrote an account of it. The original manu-script was destroyed by a fire at Westminster in 1721, but happily copies had been made beforehand. Called *The Song of Maldon*, it has been done into more modern English by H. T. Powles, so that ordinary folk may read and enjoy it. Besides giving 'the song' itself, Mr. Powles examines all the known facts, and his conclusions show us where, almost without a doubt, the famous encounter took place.

In the eighth century Maldon was fortified by Alfred's son, Edward the Elder. England was strong then, having been fairly united for a hundred years. Then came Ethelred the Unready, and ten thousand 'quid' (and money was money then) went 'down the drain' in bribes. The Danes, daily becoming more and more rapacious, descended in increasing numbers on a land, if not of milk and honey, then of mead, which is honey without the milk.

(I once made some mead to help keep the memory of Alfred alive. It failed in its object, since samples caused any thoughts of Alfred to wane. Nevertheless, it was very good, it made one feel 'brave'—the excuse a schoolboy made when chidden for reading penny 'blood and thunders'.)

After looting Ipswich, in 885, the Norsemen sailed up the Black-water and came to anchor above Heybridge, demanding ransom from the town in the approved manner of the times,

> . . . thou must quickly send
> Bracelets for ransom; and to you it better is
> That ye with gift buy off this ousel.

The Saxons had heard tales very much like this before, and the great Brithnoth had no hesitation in fighting.

> . . . we to you for gifts give spears
> The poisoned point and the old sword.

After such an exchange of ideas battle was inevitable. Mr. Powles makes it clear that it took place on the Causeway joining Northey Island to the mainland, about two miles south-east from Maldon. It exists to-day.

The invaders had established themselves on the island, so that at high water nothing but a little arrow-shooting could be done. With

94

the falling of the tide the tempo of events quickened. Three Saxons felt their way along the causeway like the trio at Rome in the 'brave days of old'. The roadway becoming uncovered, the Danes surged forward, and the battle was joined. Bravely the Saxons fought to within sight of victory when, at the crucial moment, Brithnoth, who was 'everywhere at once', fell,

> . . . wounded in the breast,
> Through to the ring mail in his heart
> Stood the poisoned point. The Earl was the gayer,
> Laughed that proud man—said thanks to his Maker
> For that day's work which the Lord had given him
> Hurled then one of the pirates a dart from his hands
> To fly from his hand, that it pierced right through
> The noble one.

So, with the striking down of Earl Brithnoth—the noble one—the end came, and notwithstanding the splendid, defiant

> The will shall be harder, the courage shall be keener,
> Spirit shall grow great as our strength falls away.

the Saxons were defeated, and the Danes possessed themselves of the town and all that part of Essex round about, establishing a great winter camp on Danbury Hill as we have seen.

In the eleventh and twelfth centuries Maldon was the chief port in Essex and prosperous. Although prosperous still, it is the chief port no longer; no more are 48-gun ships laid down, built and launched as they were three hundred years ago. But shipbuilding goes on in the form of handsome little yachts, and a picturesque working fleet of smacks still lies, when not at work, on the steep, hard riverside. Behind them, tier upon tier, buildings of all descriptions pile one upon the other, rising up and up and up to the summit of the hill, where the church of All Saints points to the skies. Of Maldon's many inns, the most interesting from an archæological point of view is the 'Blue

MALDON.

Boar'. Its outward appearance does not prepare one for the sight of the coaching yard surrounded by as fine old timbered buildings of the fifteenth century as one could wish to see.

There are really only two churches at Maldon, though there seems to be three. At the bottom of the hill St. Mary's has been over-restored and no longer supports a beacon on its tower to guide poor mariners on dark nights as it used to do. And the Church of St. Peter at the top is no church at all. The tower is there certainly, but what looks like the church itself is really Dr. Plumer's library. Opposite the 'Blue Boar' on the very crest of the hills stands All Saints' Church, with its unique and splendid triangular tower. On the south wall niches contain ably wrought figures of six of Maldon's famous men. Brithnoth is there, of course, clad in mail and looking brave as he has every right

to do: Bishop Cedde looks out upon the road he must have trod, seeing the motor-cars go by, wondering what all the bustle is about.

In the churchyard lies the body of the great-great-grandfather of George Washington, to whose memory a window was presented to the church by the citizens of the United States in 1922.

Within, besides much else of interest, is the magnificent canopied tomb of Thomas Cammock. We already know something of this masterful man and his mettlesome second wife, how they braved the wrath of an irate parent and a strong tide at Fambridge for love's sweet sake. Here they lie now, quietly, he with a wife on either side.

All round and about we see the results of his marriage—over a score of children. Twenty-two to be precise—enough for a game of cricket!

CHAPTER VI

THE BLACKWATER RIVER:
NORTH BANK

This is my own, my native land.

SIR WALTER SCOTT

ONE may still occasionally hear an old fisherman refer to the
Blackwater as the 'Pant'—its former name, and so called above
Bocking, far inland, to this day.

From the Bench Head buoy, guarding the shoal running out from
East Mersea, to the Nass, the river presents no difficulty to the sailing
man—unless it be the Cocum Hills, which lie hard and unyielding,
ever ready to receive the keel of a yacht standing too close inshore off
East Mersea church. The trick of avoiding the danger is this. When
beating, keep the easily seen sheds on Packing Shed Island clear of the
great clump of trees obscuring West Mersea church.

The Nass Beacon (*Naes*—Old English—a promontory) which was for
so many years such a familiar sea mark to east coast yachtsmen is, alas, no
longer·with us, and I often wonder where our old friend the frank heron
settles now that his perch, from which he was so fond of gazing, has gone.
Its place has been taken by a red and white spherical buoy surmounted
by a black basket on the sides of which, but upside down, the word
NASS is painted. The buoy marks the end of the long spit running down
from Tollesbury Pier and floats in under a fathom at L.W.O.S.

Old stumps on the Nass above the buoy are a danger, but two small
buoys, black and white to port, red and white to starboard, indicate
the channel.

Bound for Mersea in a vessel of any draught at all you might just as
well make up your mind to lie at the 'top o' deeps', as Mersea Quarters
are called, rowing ashore later in a dinghy. If you persevere, without

99

local knowledge you will either run aground or, having got well up one of the creeks, find no room to anchor (and precious little to turn), nor any moorings available. There is nothing for it, then, but to worry your way out to the quarters again. Of the alternatives you will very likely run ashore.

This is a 'dog in the manger' attitude to which I freely confess. I am very fond of seeing a yacht lying moored in one of the creeks, and her resplendent enamelled topsides shining in the sunshine look fine —so far! Biased I may be, nevertheless there is truth in what I say. The creeks are crowded with yachts and smacks, the channels are narrow, and there is more mud than water; but a shallow draft boat may find an anchorage somewhere along the edges of the mud with only the inconvenience of an hour or so aground. There are three hards; two in Bessom, called 'Buzz'm' by the fishermen, who are the principal users of this shallow creek; the third, a fine concrete causeway, lies off the 'Old City'.

Alongside, the firm clean foreshore is convenient for scrubbing. If a boat has received damage she can be artfully repaired or, should she require smartening up, they are 'dabsters' with the paint-brush at Mersea.

Sails can be repaired, refashioned, and dressed, or a fine new suit of

THE HILL. WEST MERSEA.

canvas made which will be a credit, not only to their makers, but also to any yacht.

Since provisions of all sorts can be bought in the nearby village, you will see at once that in this delectable place a yachtsman need want for nothing.

Mersea Island is approached by road from Colchester or Maldon over the 'Strood', which is submerged for an hour or two at spring tides. There was a ford here nearly two thousand years ago when the Romans used the island not only as a 'look-out' across the seas but also as a watering-place. Officers of the Legion built villas with tessellated pavements, which may still be seen near the church. Some left their Latin bones in the Romano-British tumuli on Barrow Hill. Later the Danes drew their long-ships up on the beach for the winter and made it a strong place.

In 895 (across the river, Cedde had been and gone these two hundred years) after one of their periodic forays they retired 'so that,' says the Anglo-Saxon Chronicle, 'the King's army could not reach them till they came into Essex eastward on an Island that is out at sea, called Mersey'. From this short contemporary note authorities have inferred that Alfred himself came to Mersea, and it may well be so.

The Danes not only contended with the Saxons, but fought among themselves. Two brothers fell in love with the same fair maiden. Who the lucky man should be could only be decided by force of arms. With their harness heavy upon them they fought hard and long throughout the day until, in the cool of evening, and spent with exertion, they fell dead side by side. The maiden, stricken with grief, could no longer support life, and the trio were buried on Barrow Hill. Those of good hearing say that when the harvest moon rises in the fullness of her glory they hear the clash of sword on sword and the clang of shield to shield. The night is disturbed by harsh cries and hard breathing. The earth trembles a little as heavy bodies strike the ground. The old ones are at it again. There is the heartbreaking wail of the lady. As the moon wanes so does the tumult die. The brothers hack at each other with decreasing fury, the wailing sinks to a whimper, becomes a sob, and then all is quiet again. But I have never heard these things.

Before the Normans came a church was built on the island, and most of the tower seen to-day is Saxon. Besides being in itself picturesque, the church is charmingly nestled between elms and great chestnut trees, and on 'high days and holidays' from the flagstaff the red cross of St. George flies bravely because the vicar likes it so.

In 1346 the island provided a barge and six men to help Edward III at Calais, and in the time of Charles I a small fort at East Mersea was occupied by the Royalists, who had vessels riding off Brightlingsea as well. A Roundhead 'mopping-up' party detached from the siege of Colchester soon reduced the little fort and took possession of the ships. Mersea went about its business, a little frightened perhaps at these goings on but, like the rest of Essex, not greatly concerned with the differences between king and parliament.

A few years later, according to Thomas Cox, the island became populous. 'This Isle,' he says, 'is a Place of great Strength, and may almost be kept against the whole world; for which reason the Parliament put 1,000 men to guard from any attempt of the Dutch in the Dutch wars.'

The island, like the whole of the Blackwater river, is famous for wild-fowling. My own experience began and ended one chilly afternoon in November, when I was sworn at for coughing at what was said to be a critical moment. I continued to cough, not only then, but for several weeks afterwards, but was cured of wild-fowling the same day. I fear I am no sportsman, and to me the game is not worth the gander.

The opening night of the shooting season is looked forward to with eagerness. At ten o'clock on the last night in September figures issue from the inns fortified by warming drinks within and a mass of clothing without. Punts have been made ready beforehand, so that it is only necessary to stow away a number of bottles (which, as at fishing, seem to be part of the ritual) and depart into the creeks, into the darkness.

On the stroke of midnight (or a moment or two before perhaps, so itchy are trigger fingers) a tremendous salvo is let loose on principle, and from then onwards spasmodic firing goes on well into the night, breaking into a fury of sound from dawn onwards until the 'flight' is over. The weary, cold, and very likely empty-handed but nevertheless still enthusiastic band comes ashore to boast of its prowess or to console itself for its non-success.

Years ago a well-known local 'gun', seeing a movement near a decoy, instantly let drive. His brother promptly sprang howling into the air to receive a second charge as he ascended. The sportsman admitted having mistaken the tail of his brother's shirt for a swan. The victim, who carried the pellets to the grave, lived to a great age and boasted when over eighty that he was as 'fit and fierce as ever'. And so he was.

He it was who, one cold and dismal winter afternoon, saw the heavy defeat of the local football eleven on their own ground at the hands of their hated Brightlingsea rivals. As the final whistle blew the dejected handful of spectators shuffled their frozen feet homewards. He, more in sorrow than in anger, blamed the moon for the dreadful catastrophe,

> Sadurd'y new and Sunday full
> Never brought good nor never ull.

This handy old rhyme serves, not only in Essex but elsewhere, as balm and solace for many and widely divergent setbacks.

Oysters fatten well at Mersea, and millions of the Portuguese variety are nourished in the creeks besides, of course, the famous Native and the American 'Bluepoint'; or did before the war. What will happen now nobody knows, but it is unthinkable that the fleet of smacks, dwindling, alas, should disappear altogether through lack of work. The industry cannot die. To see the lovely Mersea boats 'drudging' again will bring pleasure to one pair of eyes and gladden at least one heart.

Jogging along with dredge down one calm day in one of these vessels, with a reef in the main and a spitfire jib half-way along the bowsprit (as is usual, because speed is not desired but rather slowness) a lad said, 'Grand'fer', can't we shake out the reefs?' 'Blast ye boy! Do you let things be as they are. Don't yew alter nothin', there ain't enough wind for what little sail we hev got.'

No doubt the anecdote originated with the well-known Admiral William Wyatt, who has an inexhaustible fund of knowledge and wit. I said, 'If I mention you in my book shall you mind, William?' 'I don't care a damn what you say', he replied, 'so long as you don't tell the truth.' He went on to relate how once he procured a job as lady's maid for a distant relative. 'Thus good, that is,' said her mother, 'if only I can get riddy of the six gals the ten boys can look arter themselves."

A jovial octogenarian! 'Will you take a pint of beer with me. sir?' said he to an old customer.

'Thanks very much, but if I do I expect it will go down on the bill.'

'So it will if you don't, so you might just as well hev ut!'

One dark night a policeman newly come to the island asked of him his name. 'If you want to know who I am,' says William, 'ask anybody about here, they'll soon tell you, for I shan't. Good night.' He may recall how, as a boy, he looked through the windows of the old 'Victory', that one-time smugglers' haunt in the Old City, and saw Frenchmen dancing upon the sanded floor. As they danced they sang ribald songs in their native tongue, letting off the while squibs and crackers which, snapping and banging, terrified the little boy outside

with his nose to the pane. He will tell you also of days gone by when Thames 'Peter' boats came up through Havengore and the Raysand Channel to Mersea, foraging in the dead of night on Foulness Island as they came, with the consequence that many an old sheep who breathed her last was eaten as lamb on Mersea Island. There is the yarn, too, of the porpoises sunning themselves on the banks of the Ray Channel. Like mice in dinghies William and his followers made haste to take a turn round their tails. Now laughing, singing, and shouting with joy the merry crew hustled the animals into their element. Off they went towing the dinghies at a rate o' knots out to sea for a distance which lengthens with the years.

The creeks were the haunt of smugglers, and there is a 'look-out' still on a house near the church (you can see it in my drawing) from which preventive men cast a watchful eye.

To explore all the inlets round Mersea would take days, and they would be well spent. 'Ditch crawling' is good fun.

At low tide the restricted water in the creeks is calm and still, unruffled by the wind soughing across the marshes above. It reflects the sky like a mirror. Peeping over the grass-tufted edge of the saltings cumulus clouds sweep across its surface upside down. All is quiet. Even the dinghy's wash is subdued—the little waves merge into, rather than lap, the limits of the tide. High banks of glistening mud rise on either side, blue and grey and sepia, or like a pearl.

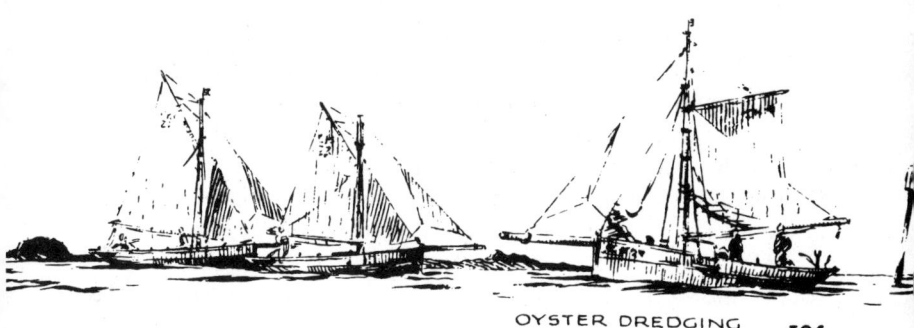

OYSTER DREDGING

Smooth in the distance but broken by many rivulets running down from the saltings, stabbed with stumps of old withies, marked by tall brooms carrying a drooping pennant of seaweeds and grasses caught when the tide was high and held aloft, the creeks amble contentedly far inland. Soon the rising water climbs steadily and quietly uphill. Withy stumps become covered, green crabs find a growing world to explore, jellyfish left high and dry feel the touch of their element again, and become water-borne. Weeds on the withies, struggling to keep the sun upon them, submerge at last, waving like sunken banners in another world. With the growing tide creeks become rivers. At springs they spread over the saltings and extend to the foot of ancient sea-walls, taking upon themselves the appearance of vast lakes.

One sails not on a level with the land but above it.

Looking from a creek over the sea-wall, masts of yachts and fishing vessels point up, their little coloured burgees waving merrily. Far off a village, caught by the sun, seems on fire, its tiled roof a blaze of light, its church tower warm-grey and mellow before a clump of elms. Beyond, across the flat indented marshes, beyond the village and blue in the distance, trees on the mainland meet the vast bowl of the sky. The silence of it all is broken perhaps by the cry of a curlew, a 'pee-wit', or the harsh 'kraak' of a heron, his wings flapping lazily as he lumbers across the saltings. Far away a dog barks. A fish 'flops' in the calm water of the creek, now at high tide still as a mill-pond, glassy, waiting—poised as it were—for the moment when it must hurry once again out to sea. The openness of it and the freedom! The cleanliness! The splendour of it all!

Take Salcot Creek for instance. With a rising tide a dinghy can twist and turn along its winding course until it comes to the little hamlet that gives it its name. That is to say, you can do so at the time of writing, but soon, just below the village, a dam is to be built across the channel to prevent flooding. I hope they will put a little stage for us to land on, so that we can still go by water to take delight in the pretty hamlet. Salcot (and I warn you to pronounce it 'Sawc't') means 'Salt Cottages'. Long ago, perhaps even as far back as prehistoric times, there were many salt-pans in the marshes, but their exact use has never been determined. Nor has the mystery of the Red Hills which abound, not only here but elsewhere on the Essex seaboard. Composed of burnt earth sometimes as high as six feet they may have been prehistoric potteries, since fragments of domestic vessels are commonly found within them.

Opposite Salcot on the other side of the creek is Virley, with its ruinous ivy-clad church so vividly described by the Rev. Baring Gould in his novel *Mehalah*. 'A small hunch-backed edifice,' he says, 'in the last stages of dilapidation, in a grave-yard, unhedged, unwalled; the church is scrambled over by ivy, with lattice windows bulged in by the violence of the gales, and a bell-cot leaning on one side like a drunkard.'

The congregation on Sundays consisted chiefly of young people. The youths who attended divine service occupied the hour of worship by wafting kisses to the girls, making faces at the children, and scratching ships on the paint of the pews—'the dearly beloveds' met in the Lord's house every Lord's Day to acknowledge their 'erring and straying like lost sheep' and make appointments for 'erring and straying' again.

Baring Gould, sometime vicar at East Mersea, understood his

parishioners but little, and they him not at all. But he understood the marshes all right and his *Mehalah* deserves to be reprinted if only for his magnificent descriptions of the Essex seaboard. They have never been equalled. The novel, moreover, is a thriller of the first order. One trembles for Mehalah, that troubled girl, living on Ray Island with her gin-sodden mother, when her house was set on fire. In bed o' nights one's hair stands end-on at the thought of Isaac Rebow keeping his brother incarcerated and manacled in the awful cellars of Barn Hall. One almost shouts (what a film it would make!) 'Don't do it,' when the iron ring slips over Mehalah's finger in Virley Church. One shudders—but there—read the book yourself if you can get hold of it, and enjoy it. With all its melodrama, through the story sings a salt-laden wind blowing across the marshes.

From Mersea turn left for Maldon at the old and picturesque (and free!) Peldon Rose—a little gem—nicely placed. Past those charming rambling farms of Essex, through avenues of elms, over railway tracks, skirting beaches, crossing a canal and a river. Through lovely villages such as Tolleshunt D'Arcy where there is an interesting church and a moated manor; where the pink-plastered houses are all awry as they are in fairyland.

One can turn off here for Tollesbury, renowned for its yacht-hands and skippers. By water one sails inside the Nass up Tollesbury Creek, skirting a forest of withies which mark a 'horse' in the middle of the channel. The creek turns northward and soon a branch to port is seen. Anchor off it if you draw a lot of water and row in in the dinghy. Land at the 'Gridiron'—a quay on the starboard hand—or else, and better still, at Drake's Yard where the foreshore is steep and hard, and where in the winter a large number of big yachts are hauled up, and a fine sight they are to be sure.

In years gone by we used to land on Tollesbury Pier and take a first-class railway ticket to the village. We never shall again. But we may pull cows out of the mud as was our wont. There one would lie in a soft patch in a creek with only her head and backbone visible.

108

TOLLESHUNT D'ARCY

At first sight it seemed impossible to do anything at all with the great heavy, awkwardly shaped animal so deeply sunk in the ooze. But once we got a stout rope over her horns it wasn't as difficult as it appeared. As we 'laid on', the neck seemed to stretch like elastic. Prodigious gurglings and the shoulders were in sight. Pools of black water became little torrents rushing into the crater formed by the now struggling cow. A tremendous last 'Heave O!' and on our backs we fell as the mud-plastered animal scrambled to her feet bellowing loudly as she trotted along the raised sea-wall. The many ropes festooned about her horns and shoulders seemed to lash the startled beast to greater exertions as, casting clots of mud in all directions from her bedaubed sides, she lumbered out of sight, to become engulfed perhaps in another creek.

The 'locals' were always highly delighted with the morning's work, 'reckoning' as they said 'to earn a crown' while we amateurs certainly earned ourselves (and paid for) a drink.

Forming the sides of the 'Square' at Tollesbury stands an assortment of plaster and brick houses variously shaped and coloured, their tiled roofs mossy and mellowed by age. On the opposite corner to the inn, and reflected in a pond when the water is not ruffled by ducks, stands the church with its squat flint tower. Go inside if only to read the inscription on the bowl of the font.

> Good people all I pray take care,
> That in ye church you do not swear,
> As this man did.

An entry in the parish register tells us how it came to be written. '*August 30th, 1718*. Elizabeth, daughter of Robert and Eliza Wood, being ye first childe whom was baptized in the New Font which was bought out of five pounds paid by John Norman, who some few months before came drunk into the church and cursed and talked loud in the time of Divine Service, to prevent his being prosecuted for which he paid by agreement the above said five pounds. Note that the wise rhymes on the font were put there by the sole order of Robert Joyce then Churchwarden!'

One can see through the years the worthy Robert, angered by the disgraceful episode yet bringing good out of evil while seeing to it that his own honourable part should not be overlooked.

While we stroll over the saltings and go aboard to sail up-river, the motorist can be jogging along the highway to Goldhanger where he will be waiting to 'have one' with us at the 'Chequers'.

Down and round the Nass we go, making for Tollesbury pier if the tide is ebbing or standing over to the other side of the river if it is in our

110

TOLLESBURY CHURCH

favour because it runs faster there. The river is deep and wide until, having passed the pier, a great shoal from the northern bank reduces it to less than half its former width. The shoal is pierced by Thirslet Creek (pronounced Thisley) which is of service to smacksmen but which should be avoided by all right-thinking yachtsmen. The shoal at its eastern end is marked by beacons and a buoy. The stream, here called 'the Ware', gathers momentum as it approaches the shoal, racing along the Ramsey side of the river at as much as four knots.

A red buoy marks the western extremity of the flats, and serves also as a starboard buoy for Goldhanger Creek in which six feet of water are to be found for a considerable distance.

Sounding is the order of the day. Leave the yacht when you have gone as far as the depth will allow and take to the dinghy. The water is remarkably clear; looking down into it one has the sensation of floating in air. In the channel the water is a deep green because of the weedy bottom—but as you cross it grey humps of mud like sleeping aquatic beasts jump up suddenly as the flats are reached. Long, brown, ribbon weed waves from the bottom, languidly twisting and turning in the tide; fishes dart like flashes of lightning from dark caves of mystery. Green crabs, running side-along across the muddy plain beneath, stop suddenly and look inquiringly upward to find out why the sunlight has left them as the shadow cast by the dinghy glides silently overhead.

Electric-blue jellyfish float along, carried helplessly yet gracefully by their master, the tide. All is cold and mysterious in this beautiful underwater world.

There can be no 'sailing directions' for Goldhanger. Just feel your way in and land at a steep-to hard. A short walk takes one to the 'Chequers' where our friends of the road await us. They have a custom in the bar, common inland, but less so on the coast. While you are waiting for your pint the old fellows offer you theirs to sip. On the arrival of your own drink it is proper to return the compliment by

going round yourself and giving them the opportunity of swallowing a mouthful also.

A nice little village with a pump. Nothing much to do except look at old-fashioned country gardens, but mighty pleasant all the same.

One can carry on by water from Goldhanger Creek through the 'Stumble' as it is called and so rejoin the main river above Osea Island, but by half ebb the roadway connecting the island dries out, preventing vessels from circumnavigating the island.

Defoe had a word to say about Osea. Old man ague rears his ugly head again.

'Ossey, or Osyth Island, commonly called Oosy Island, so well known by our London men of pleasure for the infinite number of wildfowl, that is to say, duck, mallard, teal and widgeon, of which there are such vast flights, that they tell us the island, namely the Creek, seems covered with them, at certain times of the year, and they go from London on purpose for the pleasure of shooting; and indeed often come home very well loaden with game. But it must be remembered too, that those gentlemen who are such lovers of the sport, and go so far for it, often return with an Essex ague on their backs, which they find a heavier load than the fowl they have shot.' Not much different then from now.

OSEA ISLAND.

113

Coming up-river, Osea Island resembles an atoll plucked from the Southern Seas. On a hot summer's day it often appears as a mirage floating in air, pearly-grey and lovely, shimmering in the warmth of the day. One almost expects to discover hibiscus-flowered dusky maidens, or savage men racing along the strand—or both.

The sight of the island always constrains my cousin to speak of the skipper of a schooner who sent his mate aloft with a spy-glass to make what he could of a distant tropical isle. 'What do you see?' roars the Captain. 'A lot of coconut trees and a coral reef,' bawls the mate. 'Any sign of humanity?' shouts the skipper. 'No,' cries the mate, 'all I can see is a lot of blasted niggers running about.'

The southern shore of Osea is steep-to and yachts anchor as close in as may be, so escaping the strength of the tide which runs very strongly soon after high water hereabouts in the comparative bottle-neck caused by the island.

When you land you need have no fear of savages but rather the pleasant experience of startling, or being startled by, young ladies preparing to bathe.

The large, double-fronted house standing a little way back from the beach was used at one time as a home for inebriates. The story goes that the unfortunate inmates were served with a foaming beverage, with the colour and taste of ale which grew weaker and weaker as the treatment progressed but which, like Charles the First, retained its head till the last. It will, however, gladden some to know that the 'cure' sometimes became protracted owing to the patients' discovery of caches of intoxicants placed secretly, and profitably, under bushes by men coming down river from Maldon in the darkness of the night.

A yacht may lean for a scrub against what is generally supposed to have been 'Jullaner's' old mast. 'Jullaner' was built during the last century by Mr. Bentall, an agricultural implement maker who, influenced by his trade, caused her to have a much deeper keel than was usual with yachts at the time. 'Bentall's Plough', as she was sometimes called, won many prizes and there is no doubt that her lines greatly influenced subsequent yacht designing.

Don't 'borrow' on any of the buoys which guide one to the end of, and beyond, Osea Island, for they mark the edge of the channel very strictly.

Above the Stumble the river shallows rapidly, but one can go up to Heybridge and Maldon soon after half flood. From Osea to Mill Beach is no distance at all; one may land on the sandy beach very popular for bathing when the tide is right, but you must go ashore round the bend of the river if you are short of food, to shop at Heybridge Basin.

Land anywhere above the Blackwater Sailing Club, walk along the sea-wall and you will step suddenly into the Netherlands. Here are lock gates and a canal willow-lined as in Holland. Looking up at the sky likely as not you will see the long pennant of a Dutchman streaming from a masthead, for eel boats come over from the Low Countries.

It is an interesting sight to see them unload. The hatches are taken off, exposing a well filled with thousands of eels. Long-handled forks with seven or eight long, curved, blunt-ended 'tines' are used to bring the eels out. Huge scales are set up on deck, weighted on one side, with a deep iron pail suspended on the other.

Twisting and squirming, the eels are forked from the hold into the pail, some falling on deck where, wriggling like adders, they try to find a way to the sea through the closed scuppers. The moment the pail is filled and weighed (for all is hurry and bustle), over it goes, shooting the eels helter-skelter down a canvas funnel to a punt-like box floating alongside. The lid is clamped down and padlocked, and the little craft, perforated with many small holes, is moored at some convenient place in the canal.

In this way eels are kept alive in perfect condition for almost any length of time until they are required for the market.

Business being over, the Dutchmen clomp ashore, leaving their wooden shoes outside the doors of the 'Jolly Sailor' or the 'Ship' (for

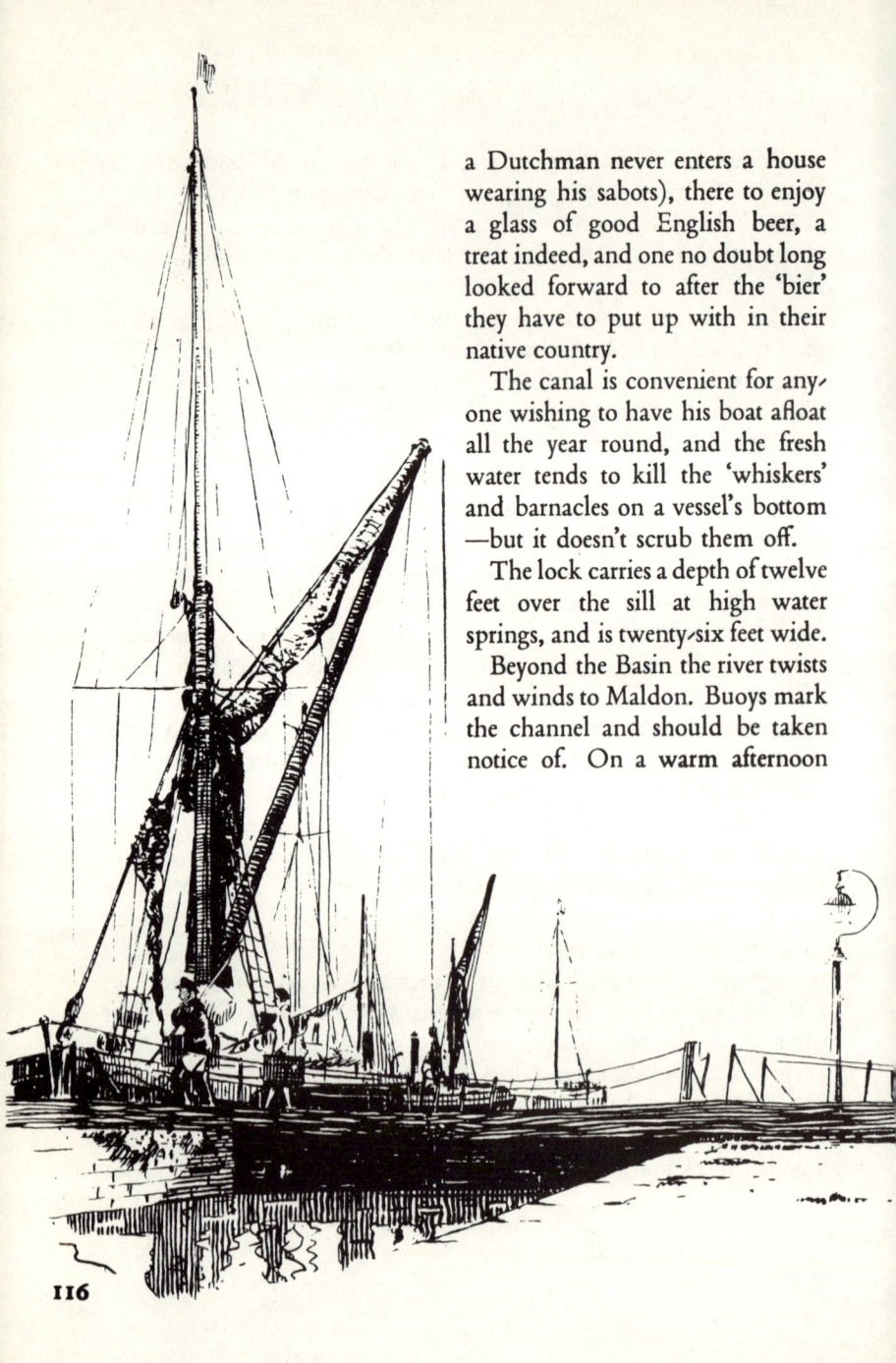

a Dutchman never enters a house wearing his sabots), there to enjoy a glass of good English beer, a treat indeed, and one no doubt long looked forward to after the 'bier' they have to put up with in their native country.

The canal is convenient for anyone wishing to have his boat afloat all the year round, and the fresh water tends to kill the 'whiskers' and barnacles on a vessel's bottom —but it doesn't scrub them off.

The lock carries a depth of twelve feet over the sill at high water springs, and is twenty-six feet wide.

Beyond the Basin the river twists and winds to Maldon. Buoys mark the channel and should be taken notice of. On a warm afternoon the river is almost impassable owing to the great number of bathers who infest the water, reminding one of the pictures one sees of multitudes of pilgrims bathing in the Ganges at Benares.

Beyond the lock which brings an end to the navigable river is Beeleigh Abbey. Established in 1180, the considerable and beautiful architectural remains of several periods are a pleasure to see. One can be shown over the building, now privately occupied, and see its treasures for a small sum which goes to the hospital. The money is, therefore, doubly spent, once on your own pleasure and again to relieve the sufferings of those less fortunate who are unable to join you.

Here, too, is a real waterfall, a rarity in Essex, and I think you should know that a sturgeon weighing one hundred and thirty-one pounds (131 lb.) is said to have been caught in the pool. No matter if the scales may not have been entirely accurate, it must have been a noble and right royal fish and I should like to have seen it.

HEYBRIDGE BASIN.

CHAPTER VII

THE COLNE

Hurrah for the Dredge, with its iron edge,
   And its mystical triangle.
And its hided net, with meshes set
   Odd fishes to entangle.
The ship may rove through the waters above
   'Mid scenes exciting wonder
But braver sights the dredge delights
   As it roves the water under.

Chorus:
Then a dredging we will go brave boys.
Then a dredging we will go.

E. FORBES

'THERE is no town in Great Britain that can compare with Colchester in the fact that it is the oldest recorded town that we know of at all in these realms.'

Such is the opinion of Sir Henry Howorth, F.R.S., and it has never been questioned.

It is, of course, hopeless to try to give in a few words more than a brief outline of this unique town's history.

What happened there in the dim Palaeolithic and Neolithic periods one can only conjecture, but there are many relics of these, and of the Bronze and Celtic periods, in the museum in the castle which is the best of its kind in Northern Europe.

Colchester's early importance was undoubtedly due to its convenience as a place of defence. The Romans established themselves on the palisaded hill, but were attacked and heavily defeated by Boadicea. Reinforced, they in turn defeated the British Queen, re-established themselves, and set about the building of a tremendous wall for their greater security. Several miles long it was and a great proportion of it remains.

Within its compass streets were laid down and houses built up. There were theatres, temples, and wine shops. Villas were centrally heated; there were public baths and every convenience civilization could provide. Britons brought to the market the produce of the soil.

At the gates in the wall the guard would turn out to inspect their credentials before allowing them to enter the town which, to the centurions, had become what might be called a 'Rome from Rome'. But Britain was Britain still, and apart from the tributes and taxes, the natives remained unaffected by their masters, absorbing none of their ways of life nor learning anything from them.

They never realized why the comparatively small body of Romans was able to keep order; they never understood the precision, manœuvrability, and efficiency of their army.

Consequently, when the legions marched away, the Britons fell an easy prey to the Saxons who came the moment Rome's back was turned. Neither did the Saxons take advantage of what must have been almost impregnable fortresses and military works all over the country.

At Colchester they left the tower of Trinity Church with its unique and lovely doorway to remind us of them, but that is all. They were unable to withstand the Vikings who left nothing at all unless it be a part of the skin of one of them to be seen in the museum. Legend says that he was 'flayed alive' at Copford for sacrilege, thus bringing everlasting, though by now greatly diminished, shame on my birthplace.

The Danes also neglected the military lessons taught by the Romans, and it was not until the arrival of the Normans that the town saw bricks and mortar used again for defence. They put the great wall in order and set about building the enormous castle, whose keep is the largest in the world and whose walls are, in parts, thirty-one feet thick of solid masonry. Once sold for one hundred pounds, it was occupied by King John and in turn by the Barons.

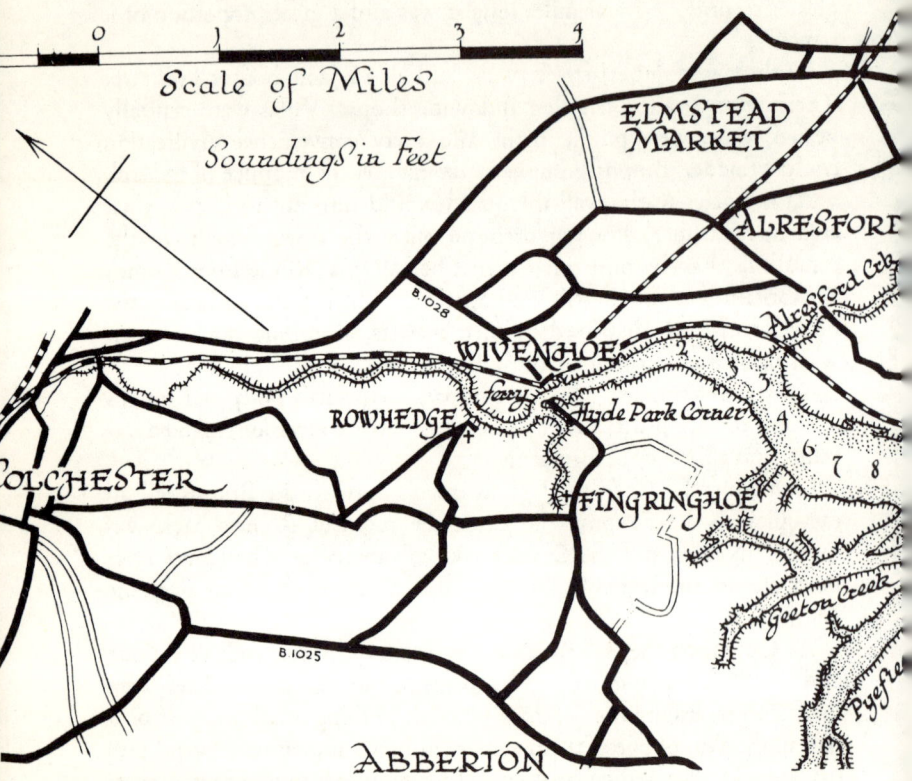

The Normans built the Priory dedicated to St. Botolph (called 'Buttles' locally), and the Abbey Gate of St. John stands pretty well as they left it.

There is the sad tale of the siege of 1648 when the Royalists defended the town for eleven weeks before surrendering. The people, having been reduced to eating horses, cats, dogs and rats, were fined the great sum of £12,000 for the trouble they had been put to. One could

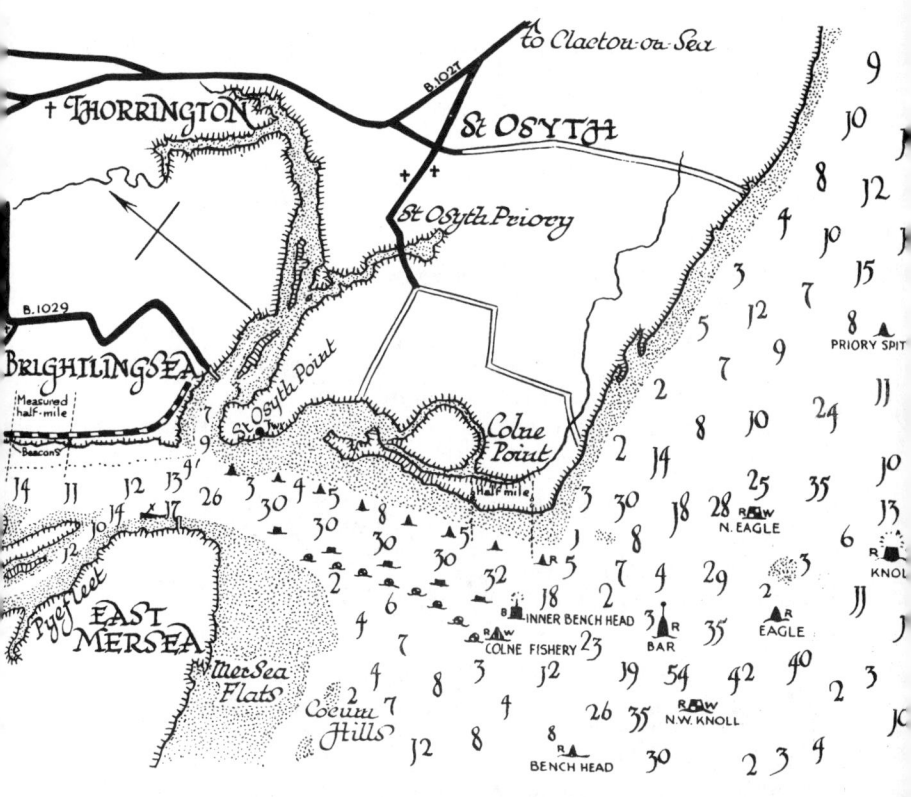

write of the plague seven years later, which struck down one in eight, and of the Huguenot era when merchants prospered exceedingly though the workers were so ill-paid that sprats were known as 'weaver's beef".

These events and much else form the background to this most ancient town, and the visitor can see in almost every street the houses in which those men of old lived.

Splendid inns have much carved woodwork, and if you would like to see the house in which 'Twinkle, twinkle, little star' was written, here it is. Do you want a pocketful of money? Take a spadeful of earth and like as not you will find a handful of coins bearing the likeness of Cunobeline. Not that they are thought much of nowadays at Colchester, where they are common enough. But if you take them to London, or some such upstart place, they will be wondered at and highly prized.

I should like to have told you about Old King Cole and his merry men, and to have had a word with you about Helen, who was a Colchester lady, and who found the True Cross. There is no room. That we have galloped through the ages, treading roughly, gives me no pleasure, for here and hereabouts is my home.

Our motoring friends have come to Colchester along the main road

COLCHESTER.

which, to tell the truth, is of little interest, and we will get them to give us a lift down to the Hythe, the town's port, where we can step aboard, leaving them to jog along through the country lanes to Brightlingsea while we 'up-anchor' at the top of high water to take the ebb down the river. At the Hythe vessels drawing as much as ten feet can lie alongside the quay, but they will dry out and it is hardly a place to leave a yacht.

Rowhedge, two or three miles seaward, was famous for its yacht skippers and remarkable for its Church of St. Lawrence. Built of white brick this octagonal architectural monstrosity is supposed to be an imitation of the chapter house of York Minster. No one questions why it was built, one can only wonder and regret that it was built that way. Nevertheless, it met with the approval of the Cranfields and Carters—names to conjure with when talk turns to the racing of yachts in the early years of the present century. They lived, and there were many of them, in the days when great long bowsprits like scaffold poles were the fashion; when booms projected like lances yards beyond the taff-rail, and tremendous jib-headed topsails were laced aloft. The slim yachts sailed on their ears, as well they might under such a press of canvas.

A Carter might be the bosom friend of a Cranfield ashore, but put them at the helm of one of the 'big-'uns', and they were, for the time being, hated enemies. Particularly at the beginning of a race when jockeying for position did the old fellows show how these fast vessels could be handled. 'Jockeying' did I say? Manslaughter would perhaps be a better description of what went on. Taunts and abuse were the order of the day. Every device they could think of to intimidate and impede their opponents was put into instant use. A favourite manœuvre was to sail down-wind at an opponent, coming about at the proper moment and letting the long boom swing over the victim's decks without touching him, for that would be a 'foul'. This piece of strategy so frightened the crew of the attacked craft that they were forced to fling themselves flat upon the decks to escape injury.

So placed, they were incapable of handling their vessel properly and were not so likely to get away with the gun. But, if they cheated, they cheated 'fair' and there were no protests unless damage was done, in which case both parties protested on principle.

In those happy days owners used very often to send their yachts across the Bay to the Mediterranean for the winter, joining her at Cannes or some such haunt of pleasure. Which brings me to the point (at last) that the Church of St. Lawrence was not to be thought of lightly. Lord Dunraven arranged for a party of his Rowhedge crew to visit St. Mark's at Venice. At the close of the day he asked his skipper's opinion. 'Well,' he said, 'what with all them domes and images I'd rather hev our owd parish church ten times over, that I would.'

On another occasion a hand was heard to remark that the Coliseum at Rome 'wanted a tidy lot done to it to put it to rights'.

Cottages all round the East Coast are filled with souvenirs of these winters in the South. Gaudy panoramas, several feet in length, of Mentone and Cannes are common; and a great favourite was a comprehensive view of the Bay of Naples at night, the moon, together with such leading and navigation lights as was proper, being brought into prominence by the cunning insertion of mother-of-pearl.

Nor were these yacht-hands afraid of putting boldly on canvas impressions of what they saw.

I was once shown, by a proud mother, a nocturne of Vesuvius in a state of chronic eruption. The town at its foot was dealt with soberly. As the eye ascended the volcano, more vivid colours were detected, until, from the jagged rim of the craters, vast vermilion and yellow flames issued, casting a horrible greenish light upon a heavy pall of smoke hanging like a blanket over the frightful scene.

In the flames and flung into stark silhouette, mighty rocks the size of taxi-cabs could be seen ascending. To the left of the catastrophe a single star, pale, green, and baleful, hung in the clouds in the southern sky. 'Young 'Arrie's father,' said the doting mother, 'did it out of his mind.'

During the latter part of the last century and the early part of this, Wivenhoe was famous for its shipbuilding and many a fine fishing vessel and many a handsome yacht went down the slipways. The industry fell into decay but was revived in 1914 and the following war years. Great was the excitement when the first of several large iron vessels was launched. Flags were flown and the town made gay. A small, wheezy tug stood by with warps handy to check the ship when she came down the 'ways'. The signal was given, the bottle broken, the chocks knocked away; down the slip the vessel came, hell for leather.

The poor little tug, first cast aside by the enormous wave and now drawn stern first, was in danger of sinking in the wake of the mighty vessel as she continued her career to 'bring up' at last athwart the stream just on high water.

There was some danger of the sea-wall's collapsing, but things were put right after a struggle. As the saying goes—it was a day!

Wivenhoe was a very favourite place for the laying up of large steam yachts, and Bayard Brown was as well known here as he was at Brightlingsea. Fabled to possess enormous wealth, this eccentric American cow-puncher was said to have been crossed in love in his youth.

The prey of innumerable sharks and cadgers, he was well able to look after himself, as he did when an enormous lady, known locally as 'the Great Eastern', received from him a bag of money. Enjoining her not to open it until she got home, Brown no doubt chuckled at his own sense of humour when he thought of the chagrin of the would-be charmer when she found the bag to be full of farthings.

Steam was constantly kept up on his large and palatial yacht, and it is said she was fully prepared to up-anchor and away to the States at a moment's notice to join his former, and by now aged, lover.

Seen from the opposite bank, Wivenhoe, as it climbs up the hill, is reminiscent of West Country waterfronts except that the reds, ochres, and russets of brick and tile give a greater and more varied warmth of colouring than does the greyness of the west.

Its fifteenth-century church contains a magnificent and intricately studded chest and three nice brasses.

In the charming little town itself much interesting 'pargetting' is to be seen on several houses.

There is not enough water in the Colne for a yacht drawing six feet to lie afloat at all states of the tide until beyond the bend in the river below Wivenhoe, known as Hyde Park Corner. One can anchor anywhere in the reach, but it is usual to bring up just above the old wreck on the East Mersea shore. Here is shelter even from the swell thrown up by a hard easterly wind.

There is a pleasant walk over the golf links to the 'Dog and Pheasant' which, I fear, is over a mile away.

WIVENHOE

The Colne from below Hyde Park Corner to the sea is comparatively deep—thirty to forty feet in parts. The Bar and Bench Head buoys mark its seaward limits, and of the two shoals they indicate, the Bar (so I am told) is the harder of the two.

From the white Colne Fishery buoy and the Inner Bench Head lighted buoy the channel is clearly marked and should present no difficulty.

Not so Brightlingsea, where the narrow channel causes the tide to run much harder than in the river, Make up for the 'Fairway' buoy at the entrance, then, judging the channel from the line of anchored boats, go in boldly and bring up as soon as you can.

Like thrusting one's head into a bag of ferrets on a dark night, it is asking for trouble to take a yacht of any size farther in than is necessary. What with the wind being 'in' when you want it 'out', and what with the wind being 'out' when you want it 'in'—what with the tide sluicing round St. Osyth Point, and what with the ferry-boats and the smacks and so on and so forth (not to mention boys) it is best to anchor at the first opportunity and have done with it, rowing in in the dinghy later, to sample the delights of the town.

I used to be prejudiced against the place. In years gone by smacks brought up to an enormous scope of chain all over the place. During the night, at the turn of the tide, they swept the channel clean, and many yachtsmen's (and women's) pyjama suits were irretrievably shrunken during wet and windy nights on deck shifting anchors in a hurry. When you went ashore hordes of boys would rush into the water and grab your dinghy before it reached the landing-stage. No sooner had you yourself set foot on the hard than your property was filled either with water, mud, and stones or with people anxious to cross to St. Osyth's Point. Before you had the chance to utter a word it was rowed away by a young imp who, charging his patrons for their journey, later charged you also for the jealously guarded privilege of 'looking after' your dinghy.

The most exasperating part of the whole business was that these young devils always called the wretched owner 'Captain'.

Things are now better ordered and one receives nothing but civility, especially from the Custom House Officers who often go out of their way to come aboard and clear a yacht quickly.

They tell me there are three hundred and eighty-eight ways of spelling Brightlingsea. 'Wrythlngseye' was moulded in the course of time to 'Brellsey' by the Admiralty, from which it would seem that

128

almost any word you care to think of can be made to spell 'Brightlingsea'.

Dr. E. P. Dickin, whose history of the town is probably the most exhaustive local history in existence, rightly castigates those who call the place 'Brittlesea.' You will never hear a local inhabitant call it anything but Brightlingsea. It is a corporate body of the Cinque Ports, being a 'limb' of Sandwich, and the ancient ceremony connected with the honour is held every year in the tower of the parish church.

The church is handier for mariners than worshippers. Since it stands on the summit of a hill its tower provides an excellent sea-mark, but since it is a mile and a half from the town it also provides a 'tidy step' for worshippers on a snowy winter's night.

For her existence Brightlingsea depends upon three industries: yachting, spratting, and oysters.

There are large and excellent yards to build and take care of yachts, and the fitting out and sailing of them give employment to many during the summer months. When the days of pleasure afloat are over and the cold autumn and winter advances the Brightlingsea man turns up his coat collar and goes stowboating, or 'stowb'tin' as the garnering of sprats is called.

They are caught in a peculiar way by a net, sometimes three hundred yards long, attached to the bows of the anchored smack; Frank Carr in his *Vanishing Craft* gives an interesting and detailed account of the procedure. The landing on the hard of hundreds of tons of sprats is one of the sights of the East Coast.

The work takes the fishing boats as far as the mouth of the Thames, but the Wallet, off Clacton, is a favourite and more convenient place.

The cultivation and marketing of the oyster is the third industry, for here the Colchester Natives, or 'Pyefleets', are reared. 'Pyefleets' are reckoned by connoisseurs to be the most succulent oyster in the world; they command very high prices, and an ordinary man might very well go through life without ever swallowing a Native unless he should

be so fortunate as to be invited to the Colchester Oyster Feast, where he may eat as large a number as he can for nothing.

At a Feast years ago a gentleman swallowed eleven dozen, while a knight once confessed to having disposed of thirteen and a half dozen at a sitting, 'Feeling', as he said at the end of the ordeal, 'ready for a few more.' Whether he meant just a 'few' more or just a few dozen more I dared not ask. This gargantuan and shameful exploit, I hasten to add, was undertaken at his own expense; the feat to-day would bring about the financial ruin of all but a millionaire—certainly of a knight.

BLUEPOINTS

Although they cannot compete with the Native in either succulence or price, 'Bluepoints' and 'Portuguese' oysters have a considerable sale. The American 'Bluepoints,' while larger and less expensive, more nearly resemble the Native than do the cheaper, rock-like 'Ports'.

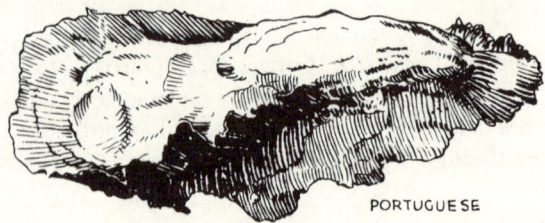

PORTUGUESE

Previous to the Oyster Feast officials and their friends have a preliminary 'taster' aboard the Company's boat in Pyefleet Channel. The first dredge of the season is hauled and found to contain oysters whose fatness is as never before, whose quality surpasses last year's samples which themselves were the best within living memory.

The same tale is told, and will be told, year after year, and great would be the consternation were the dredge to be hauled up empty. But it never will be. Gin and gingerbread, the traditional accompaniment of the oyster, is swallowed and the season declared to be 'open'. None of the oysters eaten is less than five years of age, because it takes that time to reach the size of the oyster, beautifully modelled in silver, which the Colchester Corporation keeps as the standard below which none may be sold.

NATIVES

The oyster cannot move of its own accord and, although great care is taken of its life, it is constantly assailed by a great variety of enemies and lucky to live to attend the oyster feast.

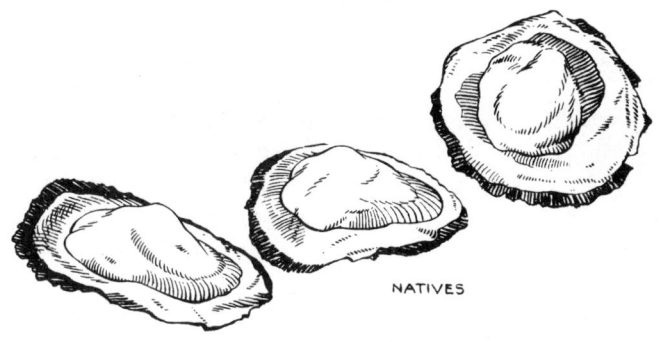

NATIVES

Whelk tingles bore into its shell to drink its bluish blood. Starfish fasten on to its valves and pull until the shell opens and the oyster within meets its doom. Slipper limpets smother it and crabs attack the weak. Seaweed stifles, heat destroys, and coldness brings about its death. No sooner is the oyster born than it is trapped for life if it is to live. It happens this way.

In the breeding season, from about May to September, oystermen put down in convenient places in the river clean shells, called 'culch', to which the oysters may cling.

Having been born, the embryo oyster, carried hither and thither by the tide for about three weeks, may, together with millions of others, and quite by chance, fasten itself to the 'culch'.

If the 'culch' is missed it suffocates in the mud. It is reckoned that a single oyster becomes the mother of about a million children each season. Of this large family only twenty or so become attached to 'culch' and of the twenty only three live to die properly at table. Bookies would class it as a rank outsider.

In infancy the oyster is known as 'spat', and the laying of the 'culch' at the proper time calls for sound judgment, being perhaps the most important operation in the oyster's culture. If it is laid too early the shells become covered with mud; if too late then the 'spat' is missed. The time of the 'fall' varies according to the temperature of the sea water. After a mild winter and a warm spring spatting will be early, if the spring is cold then it will be delayed.

In its first year the oyster increased little in size, but from then until three years old, when it is known as 'brood', the shell grows rapidly. In their fourth year, and now looking something like oysters, they are moved to fattening beds nearer inshore. The fifth year sees them fully matured and ready to die.

The reason why the Colne is especially noted for its oysters is that the combination of clean water, proper temperature, and peculiar fattening qualities seems to exist here to a greater degree than anywhere else.

So far I have referred to the oyster as 'it'. One can do little else when talking of a 'he' which, before he knows where he is, is a 'she'.

Although it is thought that all are males when born, oysters frequently change their sex. Not that they get much excitement out of it since they are brainless, headless, and limbless. All these creatures can do is to remain where they are put, open and close their shells to emit and draw in the sea, the while getting fat for the Colchester Oyster Feast, or some other occasion.

Having previously, as we have seen, whetted their appetites and whistles afloat beforehand, in October, officials of the Fishery Company have a proper sit-down feast at the Mayor of Colchester's expense. The large Moot Hall is crammed as full as it can be with friends and eminent personages.

The feast was held as far back as 1667, and has to-day become of great importance not only as a meal but also as a feast of oratory, learning, reason, and wit. Of beauty too, since the ladies, who have eaten privately in another place, come in when the dishes are cleared away to hear what their other, and by now mellow, halves have, in their wisdom, to say.

But even as the captains of industry, famous authors, soldiers, diplomatists, artists, statesmen, and other great figures are departing, even before the evening papers are out with the headlines, the men of Brightlingsea are at work clearing the beds and attending to the preparation of the oyster for next year's table. The vessels they use

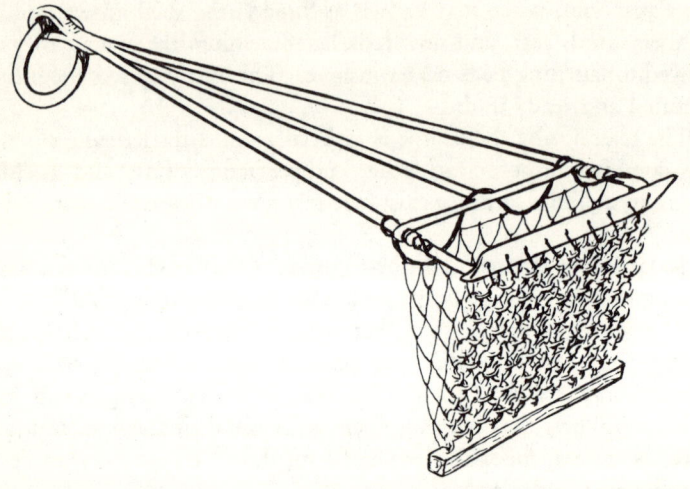

deserve a mention. Between thirty and forty feet long, with a beam of ten feet or more, they draw between five and five-feet-six.

They are cutter-rigged with a loose-footed mainsail. The straight stem rounds at the deep forefoot to a long keel, and a pretty sheer runs from the high bows to the low, flat counter stern.

The larger vessels which were used for work farther afield carried a top-mast, but the true dredgerman never needs one. The short pole mast, set well into the boat, has no cross-trees, no backstays and no fore topmast stay. The bowsprit likewise is simply rigged with only a bob-stay. The vessels when at work on the grounds are hove-to, or almost so, and make a very picturesque sight drawing slowly ahead with their 'spitfires' a-weather half-way along the bowsprit, their tanned mainsail rucked at the peak. The dredges, or 'drudges', as they are more fittingly called, are worked on rope warps from the quarters, two or more at a time being dragged gently along the bottom. Directly one is hauled aboard the contents are emptied on deck and over go the

134

dredges at once. The 'culch' to which the 'spat' has clung, is quickly sorted and stored in shallow wooden pans, the 'dross' flung overboard and the next dredge hauled. The work is therefore hard and continuous. The dredges are as alike as two peas, having arrived at their present shape through years of experience. They have not changed within living memory and never will now. (We said the same of anchors, but they have!)

The dredge is difficult to describe, but the drawing should give the reader an idea of its structure.

The iron base 'hoes' the 'culch' into the net, the underpart of which is chain to withstand wear, while the upper portion is ordinary netting easily replaceable or mendable and not subjected to the drag along the bed of the river.

In years gone by Brightlingsea men went far afield. Down channel as far as the Scillies for scallops and across to Terschelling for oysters. They went in very much larger vessels than those we have just discussed, vessels specially built for the job. High bowed, with powerful shoulders and running to over sixty feet in length with a beam somewhere round about seventeen feet, they were fitted with wells in which oysters were kept alive.

They were away a month or more at a time, according to the weather. The Dutch coast off Terschelling Light may be a very healthy place in one sense, but it was far from being so in another when the north-easterly gales came on in winter-time bringing with them rain, sleet, hail, and snow. A man wanted a good vessel under him during the dark days and nights on that inhospitable lee shore, and he had it in the 'Skillingers' as they came to be called. These great upstanding vessels were able to put up with more than man could stand. It has been stated that the men in them never went ashore from the time they left Brightlingsea until they came back. Many of them would be better off to-day had such been the case, but it was not so. 'Look at that owd feller there', said another 'owd fellow' to me. ''Im 'n me 've played up the devil over there at 'Skelling—played up the

THE LAST OF THE 'SKILLINGERS'

devil we hev many a time—used to set 'em alight over there that we did.'

I could draw no further explanation from him, but at the mention of 'Bols' a faraway look came into his eyes, a wisp of a smile spread over his gnarled and weather-beaten face, and in perfect accord we entered the 'Anchor'. Yes! They were the boys! They feared nothing, alive or dead. Great big men they were, and are still. They say a Yorkshireman will take a tin of sardines, clap it between a couple of slices of bread, call it a sandwich and eat it that way. It is a habit they have too at Brightlingsea, except that they don't cut the crust off the bread.

But the days of going offshore are over and the few remaining 'Skillingers' are drawn up ashore and rotting away. We shall never see again the big smacks with their top-masts, beating up Tollesbury Fleet or into Brightlingsea; nor shall we ever behold the sight of them threshing up the Colne in a breeze, to bring up like thunder, head to wind and stand still alongside the quays of Wivenhoe and Rowhedge.

Those were the days of sail and they are gone. But we had better step ashore and join our motoring friends who, while we have been ruminating as we jogged down the river, have also been coming along, branching off at Wivenhoe Park to have a look at Wivenhoe, and perhaps have crossed the Colne in the ferry-boat to see the wall-painting in Fingringhoe Church, which shows St. Michael computing the weight of souls, meditating the while on the wickedness of the smugglers who are said to have used the church as a rum store. Then back and on the old road, up hills and down dells, with glimpses through the trees over the river and creeks to Brightlingsea.

Let us have tea at Jacobs Hall,

THE TOPIARY ST OSYTH

137

a delightful half-timbered, Early Tudor house, once the home of the Beriffs, rich merchants and shipowners who helped to build the parish church so far from the town. Its handsome flint-faced tower is one hundred feet high, and reminds us of the Suffolk and Norfolk churches. It has a great number of niches, several brasses to the Beriffs family, and a monument to Nicolas Magens, which cost, they say, £6,000. On the walls are many plaques showing how great has been the number of men the sea has taken from the town. Beyond the church we must turn to the right at the main road past Thorington to St. Osyth village where you have before you the splendid façade of St. Osyth Abbey. I say 'Abbey' because Abbey it is and not a Priory as it is usually called.

It is true that in the twelfth century a priory was founded at 'Chich', St. Osyth's ancient name,   Becoming rich it was converted into an Abbey dedicated to SS. Peter, Paul, and Osyth. Suppressed in 1539 it was an abbey at the time and should really be so called.

The gatehouse seen across the lawn is a beauty. Elaborately panelled in flint and stone, behind it can be seen the old Abbot's Tower similarly faced. For a small sum, at certain times in the summer, one has the privilege of walking in the beautiful grounds. As at Beeleigh, the money goes to an hospital; no names are taken, so one does good by stealth. Inside you may see more closely the Abbot's Tower and a magnificent oriel window. Here are lovely flower-beds set amid smooth lawns. There are fishponds, and in another part a nice example of the topiarist's art which I have drawn as well as I can. The abbey they say is haunted by the ghost of St. Osyth. Perhaps Osyth was the daughter of Frithewald, a 'King' of Mercia, over against Wales.

However that may be she founded the Priory of Chich in 673.

Notwithstanding a vow of virginity Osyth found herself married to Sighere, a King of Essex. At the wedding feast report came that a stag had been sighted. Thereupon Sighere sprang from table to horse, followed by his men, thus forming a 'stag' party.

'Hunting he loved, but love he laughed to scorn.'

Osyth took the opportunity to nip away into Suffolk where she took the veil. This turn of events, which might be described as 'staggering', in no wise upset Sighere; he very magnanimously presented Chich to his virgin bride, who thereupon founded the Priory, and became Abbess of it.

Things went quietly for her and her ladies until, as Fuller in his *Worthies of England* says: 'The Danes, infesting the sea coasts, cut off her head in hatred of her religion. Yet this her head, after it was cut off, was carried by Saint Osyth (Oh, wonder. Oh, lie!) three furlongs, and then she fell down and died.' Where she fell a spring, famous for its curative powers, issued from the ground. Monks who came later

ST OSYTH MILL

built a monument to her memory and caused the water to be conveyed through a leaden pipe. So it ran until (it has been said) the pipe itself was conveyed away (Oh, wonder. Oh, lie!) by a visiting yachtsman for ballast. They say the tragic figure still walks amid the trees in silvery moonlight, singing a plaintive air, her head held before her in wan and ghostly hands. But I have never seen her.

Beyond the Abbey, in a house in the street leading to Osyth Creek, there used to be the grisly spectacle of the supposed remains of a prehistoric man, but I could not find it. In any case it is not far down the road to the ancient and picturesque tidal mill at the head of the creek. But, alas, the structure is feeling the effects of its great age and much money will have to be spent on its aged timbers if it is to stand four-square to the four winds of heaven and be a delight to the eye much longer.

CHAPTER VIII

WALTON BACKWATERS AND
THE STOUR

For while the tired waves, vainly breaking,
Seem here no painful inch to gain,
Far back, through creeks and inlets making,
Comes silent, flooding in, the main.

ARTHUR HUGH CLOUGH

BETWEEN the Colne and Dovercourt Bay there is little to detain
the yachtsman unless it be the Colne Bar or the Eagle Sands, but
we will pass them over. There are no harbours to poke into, no little
creeks to explore, although the course of a small river which ran into
the sea at Holland Gap can still be traced. In Saxon times it was owned
by a man named Gunner, whom we remember when we see 'Gunfleet' Sands printed on our charts. It was to mark these sands that 'Ye
buoy of ye Gunfleet' was laid down in 1628, the first sea-mark ever to
be placed off the Essex coast. The land, which at Colne Point is, if
anything, below sea-level, gradually rises to the height of a proper cliff
at Walton on the Naze.

For the motorist there is Clacton, striving to rival Brighton; beyond
is Frinton striving to rival Hollywood. Farther on still Walton strives
to rival nowhere at all. Nor need it. It is unrivalled, providing
relaxation for old and young. Ancients enjoy prodding the cliffs for
fossils much older than themselves. The middle-aged sun themselves
lazily on the sands or bring about a healthy tiredness by golfing in the
invigorating air on the cliffs near the Tower. The young play at
cricket, disport themselves in the warm sea or sail out to the West
Rocks where lobsters like to live. The very young prod the sands for

141

treasures cast ashore by the tide, bending little backs, gravely concen-
trating on work every bit as important as the labours of their grand-
sires stretched at the face of the cliff.

Not only has Walton a sea-front but the water comes to her back
door as well. The Backwaters, as they are called, provide capital
anchorage, and yachts of deep draught can lie afloat at all states of the
tide.

Since they are almost completely land-locked, no matter from which
direction the wind blows all is quiet and comfort. Although once
inside there is plenty of water, the entrance off Dovercourt is shallow
with but four feet at low water ordinary springs. The channel runs
between the mainland and the Pye Sands, which extend from the
Naze itself. They dry out and are hard.

The channel, roughly south-west by west, has been excellently
buoyed by the hospitable Walton and Frinton Yacht Club, and there
should be few navigational difficulties.

Perhaps when one is coming in with the sun setting ahead the marks
are sometimes not easy to pick up at once, but the Yacht Club cannot
be blamed for that. Inside the land two courses are open. Firstly, keep
on a south-westerly course for Hamford Water, a comparatively broad
channel having twenty feet at low water ordinary springs. Anywhere
here, or in Kirby Creek half a mile or more past Island Point buoy,
one may anchor in solitude. Few think of these secluded parts where
thousands of birds mate, nest, rear their young and depart to return
again the following year. Tides flow in and out cleanly. The sun sets
in all its glory over marshes unsullied by smoke. Fish flop startlingly,
'ringing' the quiet waters. Lonely places these, yet full of charm and
life for those who have the eyes to see and the mind to understand.

Secondly, bear south-south-east at the Island Point buoy up Walton
Channel. Narrower than Hamford Water, the channel has a pretty
regular depth of a couple of fathoms all along its length until, just past
the Twizzle where it turns abruptly to the westward, it gradually
shallows.

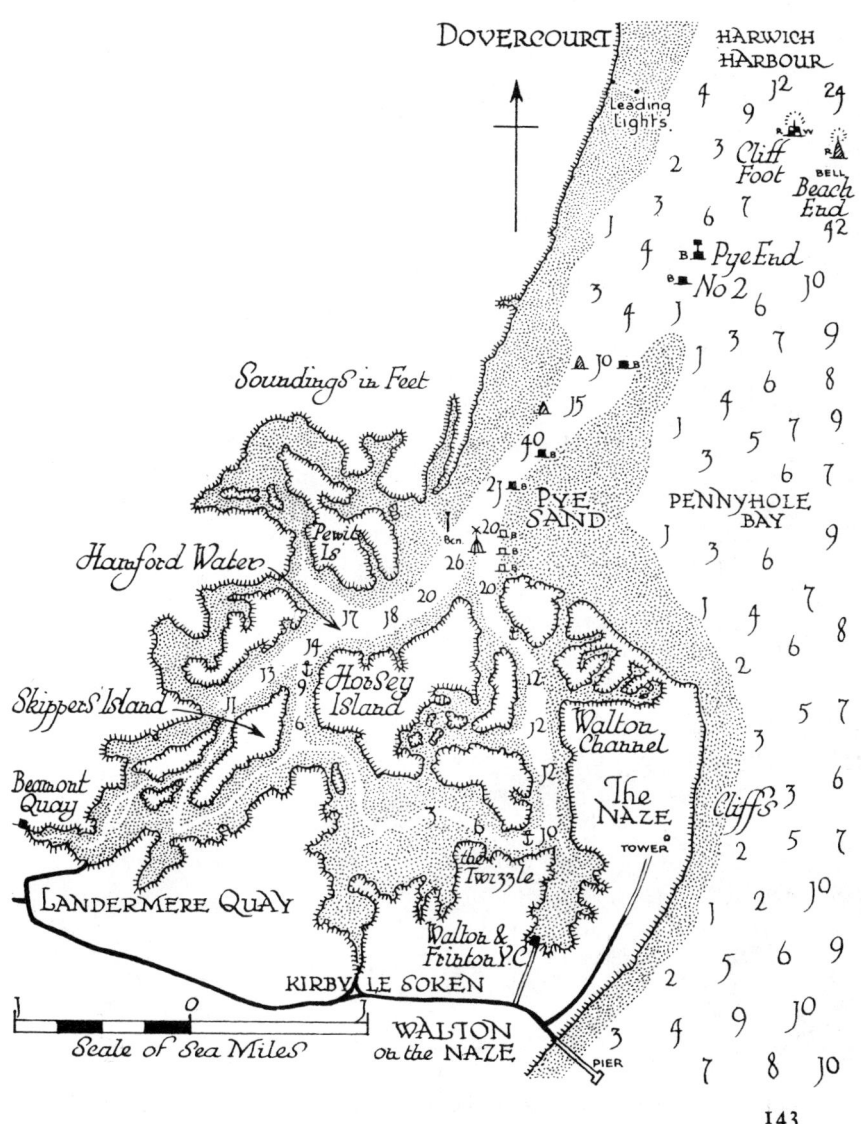

DOVERCOURT

HARWICH
HARBOUR

Leading
Lights.

Soundings in Feet

Harnford Water

Pewit
Is.

Bcn

PYE
SAND

Cliff
Foot

Pye End

No 2

BELL

Beach
End

PENNYHOLE
BAY

Walton
Channel

Horsey
Island

Skippers Island

Beaumont
Quay

The
NAZE

TOWER

Cliffs

the
Twizzle

LANDERMERE QUAY

Walton &
Frinton Y.C.

KIRBY LE SOKEN

WALTON
on the NAZE

PIER

Scale of Sea Miles

143

One can anchor off Walton Stone landing at all states of the tide to bathe from the sandy beach, as one can see from my drawing.

At the Twizzle there are many moorings, but there is generally room for a berth a little way up the creeks. Foundry Reach, an offshoot south of the main channel, has a landing place at the old Yacht Club hard, a steep to beach convenient for dinghies. From it a short walk along the sea wall brings one to the shops and ice creams. By courtesy of the Walton and Frinton Yacht Club one can land on the quay farther up and, although the tide leaves a little early and comes back a trifle late, it is handy enough for any reasonable person. Again a short walk (passing the

largest boating lake in the country) takes one to the shops (and ice-creams.) To the promenade also, from the solidarity of which it is convenient in stormy weather to 'see what it's like outside' without the trouble of going out to sea.

Walton is in the Tendring Hundred, that area which occupies the north-eastern part of Essex extending roughly from Colchester to the coast, and bounded by the rivers Colne and Stour. It has no history. No battles have been fought therein. Out of it have come no great figures striding with a noise like thunder across the receding footlights of time. The people, having been allowed to live in comparative quiet, are therefore to be envied. Nor are there any topographic features of any note. There are few shady lanes, such a characteristic

STONE POINT

of the Essex and Suffolk scene, and the few trees (fine elms though they be) are dotted higgledy-piggledy about the countryside with little distinction.

Yet it could not always have been so. Notice the village names—Mistley, Bromley, Bentley, Oakley; Weeley—how they all end in 'ley', meaning 'a woodland' or 'a clearing'. Bromley is the 'broom clearing', Bentley the 'bent-grown clearing', Mistley the 'mistletoe wood', and Oakley the 'oak clearing'.

Thorpe-le-Soken is the last resting-place of the famous Kitty Canham whose strange, sad, and true history is so well set forth after great research by Sir W. Gurney Benham. To whet the reader's appetite for the book let me say that on a night in June 1752 a small vessel anchored below Colchester. From her several large chests were landed. Williams, a young French-speaking man, greatly agitated, landed also. Smuggling being rampant at the time one can easily imagine the glee of the Customs officers when on opening the chests they saw great quantities of jewellery and the many splendid, dainty, and silken clothes of a lady.

But one box Williams would not consent to have opened. It contained, he said, the body of his wife. Half-demented, he instantly attacked an officer who had threatened to run the case through with a sword, but was overcome and held prisoner. The lid was lifted. Within, even as Williams had said, reposed the embalmed body of a most beautiful woman. Murder!

That night the corpse was lodged in the parish church at the Hythe at Colchester. The now frantic husband spent several days and nights with the body, all the time protesting his innocence. At least so far as his listeners could judge, but none could speak French. Meanwhile, the strange events becoming publicly known, a great number of people filed into the church to see the wretched prisoner and the body.

At last the mystery was cleared up. A man was found who, reasoning with Williams in his own tongue, drew from him the confession that he was none other than Lord Dalmeny. He had met this beautiful woman four years before; the couple fell in love, married, and went abroad on a protracted honeymoon. At Verona the lady fell into a decline and died.

Immediately before her death she confessed to being the wife of the Reverend Henry Gough of Thorpe-le-Soken, and begged at the same time that her body might be taken there for burial. So it came about that the French ship arrived in the Colne with so much mystery.

The Reverend Henry Gough at once recognized the body as that of his wife—Kitty Canham. Beside himself with rage he threatened the life of the noble lord. Nevertheless, when the lovely lady was at last interred at Thorpe, Dalmeny and he walked side by side behind the coffin.

Tiring of a quiet rural life Kitty Canham had run away to London, there to meet Lord Dalmeny. Rather than forgo the chance of a happier life, she kept her previous marriage secret and became his wife.

Dalmeny, who never remarried, survived her only four years, but the Reverend Henry Gough lived for a further nineteen.

One hundred years before these romantic happenings, and not ten miles away, Matthew Hopkins was busy discovering witches. Hopkins, who first practised as a lawyer, had a man named John Sterne to assist him, together with a woman 'searcher'. Setting up business in his home town of Manningtree he made a good start with seven or eight witches who, he said, met every Friday to offer sacrifices to the devil. According to him, dogs vanished at their behest. They controlled 'imps' named 'Jamara' and 'Vinegar Tom'. Another was called 'Griezzell Greedigut', a name, said Hopkins, no mortal could invent. The wretched women were bound cross-legged on a table. The door of the room was locked, with a hole bored for 'imps' to enter.

Two or three days without food or water and the victims, after being marched about briskly, were in a condition to confess almost anything. They even admitted the existence of 'Griezzell Greedigut', were 'swum,' and duly paid the penalty.

It was the popular belief that if a witch whose thumbs had been tied to her toes was thrown into a pond floated, she was guilty and hanged. If the poor wretch sank she was innocent! She therefore stood no chance. 'Near-witches' caused popular merriment on ducking-stools, not only women but men as well. John Lowes, one-time Vicar of Brandiston in Suffolk, in his eightieth year was accused of being 'allied to Satan'. His tormentors, following the Manningtree style, kept him awake for days on end, with sharp walks to follow. They then dangled him in a pond. The poor old fellow at last confessed to owning a couple of 'imps', one of which he had sent to sea to sink a ship! Before they hanged him at Framlingham he was made to read the burial service for his own benefit.

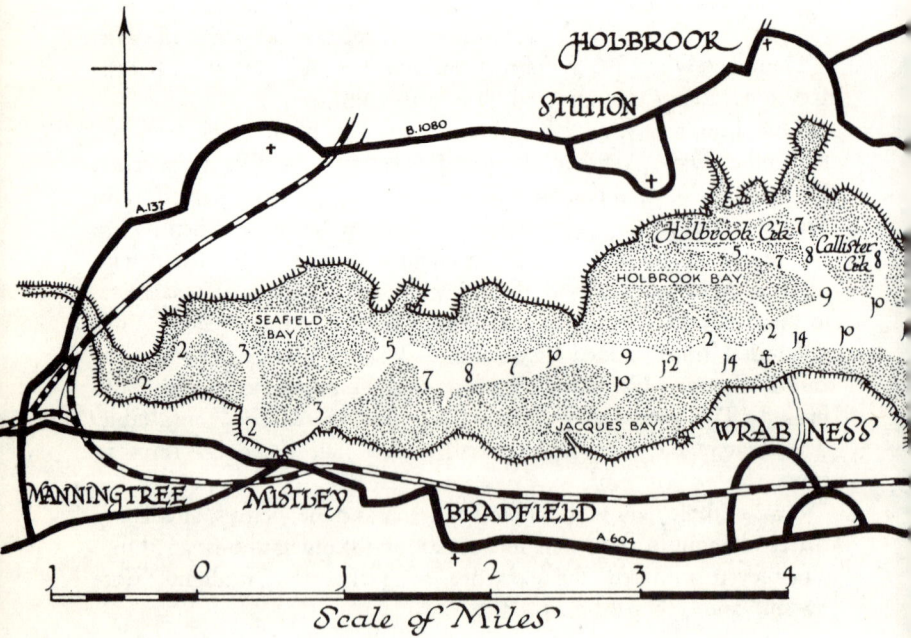

As Hopkins 'got on' in his profession he assumed the style of 'Witch-finder Generall'. His business being in the nature of 'piece-work', the more he 'found' the richer he became—it paid him to catch witches. It paid him at the rate of twenty shillings a head. The times were all awry and it is strange to think of towns asking for his assistance, paying him for his 'services'. I suspect Hopkins began to earn money too easily, for after a career of three strenuous years he wrote a pamphlet defending himself. Some authorities say he died in bed, others will have it that his thumbs were tied to his toes, he was 'swum', found guilty and hanged. At any rate he was buried at Mistley on the 12th of August 1647. But if the belief in witchcraft has not entirely gone from the world at least it has from Manningtree, where one looks in vain on windy nights for the sight of witches on brooms riding a

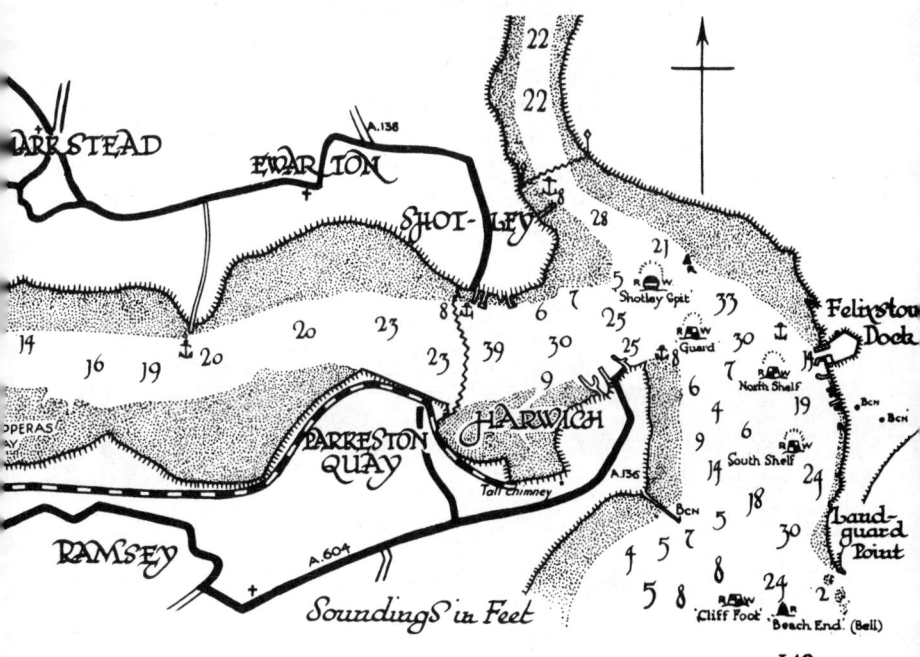

storm-wracked sky. Much more profitable to lie smoking a pipe on the greensward of the picturesque little town looking across the river Stour at the good Suffolk land rising gently, wooded and satisfying.

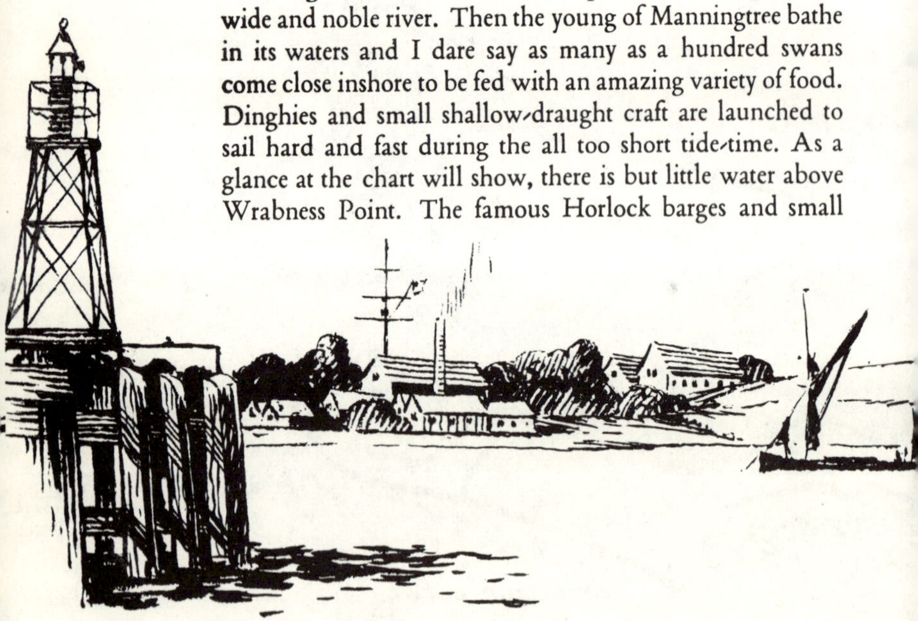

At high water the Stour takes upon itself the aspect of a wide and noble river. Then the young of Manningtree bathe in its waters and I dare say as many as a hundred swans come close inshore to be fed with an amazing variety of food. Dinghies and small shallow-draught craft are launched to sail hard and fast during the all too short tide-time. As a glance at the chart will show, there is but little water above Wrabness Point. The famous Horlock barges and small coasters trade to Mistley; otherwise the water is bare of craft. More's the pity for it is a beautiful river.

We must be content then with fourteen foot of water and a landing at any state of the tide at Wrabness Pier, a charming, unpretentious place. The little cliffs look inviting from afloat while the magnificent and imposing Naval Training School at Holbrook gives distinction to the far Suffolk shore.

Another anchorage I like to frequent is at Erwarton Ness where there is a quay for barges. Lower down still one can anchor close in to Shotley Pier in between four and five fathoms of water, deep for these parts, with a consequently steep-to beach. The disadvantage here is the procession of steamers whose departure from Parkeston Quay at ten or thereabouts in the evening seems always to coincide with the time for going aboard—and the wave they put up looks formidable from a dingy. I always think of Chesterton's

> We did not see so clear
> The night we went to Bannockburn by way of Brighton Pier.

The incoming procession staged on Sunday mornings is more useful, serving as it does to awaken sleepers who have a tide up to Mersea or Burnham to catch. On the Essex side at Harwich the 'Pound' bounded

SHOTLEY   151

on two sides by piers and sheltered by the gigantic Great Eastern Hotel, is not at all to be recommended for a yacht. Far better to anchor just inside the Guard buoy in a fathom and a half—a much more sheltered and convenient anchorage than it looks. One can land on the steps on the quay or on the beach near the ancient hulk ashore. But before I begin, as I shall, to praise Harwich (thus making this book unique since no one has ever had a good word to say for the town) I would like to advise those who come by road from Manningtree not to miss Ramsey Mill. In a capital state of preservation it is working still—on rough stuff, I fear, but all is grist to the mill; that it is working at all is something to be thankful for.

Just before Harwich is reached, Dovercourt, nowadays a rising watering-place, is renowned both for the quality of its air and for its tremendous number of hours of sunshine (aren't they all!) Years ago it was renowned for a Holy Rood, greatly venerated as having miraculous powers. The beam which supported it is still in the Church of All Saints.

Let Thomas Cox, writing in 1700, tell the story.

'Robert King, Robert Denham, Nicholas Marsh being troubled in Conscience at the Great Resort of the People to worship the Rood

at Dovercourt, whose Power they were persuaded was so great, that no Man could shut the Church Door where he stood and so imputed the Power of God to an Idol, were moved by the Spirit of God to go in a very bright night to the Place, and taking the Idol from its Shrine, burnt it.'

The affair occurred in 1532, when Henry VIII was king and men were pretty fierce in the matter of religion. It is not therefore surprising to read: 'After Great Inquiry and Search they were apprehended and being indicted of a Felony were hanged in chains. Robert King at Dedham where he and Nicholas Marsh dwelt, Robert Denham at Cattaway Cansey, and Nicolas Marsh at Dovercourt.'

One other thing about Dovercourt (besides the saying, true also of other places, that there they are 'All speakers and no hearers') is the quaint account by William Harrison in 1587 of the Dovercourt Elms.

'Of all the elms that ever I saw, those in the south side of Dovercourt, in Essex, neere Harwich are the most notable, for they growe (I meane) in crooked maner, that they are almost apt for nothing else but navie timber, great ordinance and beetels; and such thereto is their natural qualitie, that being used in the said behalfe, they continue longer, and

HARWICH.

153

more long than aine the like trees in whatsoever parcell else of this land, without cupher, shaking or cleaving as I find.'

Dovercourt, bereft now of its elms, merges into Harwich. Harwich —'a pitiful example of a decayed port, a half-ruined town of narrow, dismal streets, honeycombed with squalid alleys.' Notwithstanding the description of the town given in a local handbook I say I like Harwich, I always have liked it, and I expect I always shall, even if I have to withstand a charge of pigheadedness.

Perhaps it is because a little boy on a paddle steamer from Ipswich saw the river Orwell suddenly broaden out and beheld for the first time the Harwich skyline. From inside the harbour details of the town were hidden, the sun behind throwing it into shadow and silhouette. There was the lighthouse on the gently sloping beach. On the water-front houses of all sizes, shapes, and colours huddled together in picturesque confusion. Farther on, the Railway Hotel raised its gaunt bulk. In the background like a forest were the masts, spars, and funnels of many ships and the great lanterns of light vessels which habitually came to refit. Above, the tower of Harwich church, tall and impressive, like a dagger pointing to heaven, added dignity to the scene. That Harwich skyline of my childhood days so stands to-day, impressing me still. Perhaps ashore the shops have not the opulence of Bond Street but they are full of charm. Behind their bow windows are things not ordinarily seen. Sacks of old-time ship's biscuits, for example, made on the premises. Take some aboard. If your crew complain of hunger, give them one; it will either cure the complaint or they will put up with the hunger. (Hinged together, the delicacies make excellent folding chart-tables.)

Licorice pipes with tiny red sweets in their bowls to represent fire are still sold. I saw a notice stuck in a toffee-apple which read, 'Cash Price 1d.', and over a Mr. Cannes' shop is a petrol tin. They like a bit of humour at Harwich. There you can pick up a lobster or a crab 'very reasonable', or a quart of shrimps hot from the boiler.

The place is full of maritime history. Hereabouts in 884 the Saxons

154

fought the marauding Danes; Alfred himself was very probably there. Certainly Edward III sailed from the harbour to defeat the French at Sluys. Henry VIII graced the place with his presence, as did Good Queen Bess twenty years later when she was entertained in lavish style. Too lavish perhaps. Because, although praising the town, she granted it no favours saying 'a pretty little town and wants nothing'.

A HARWICH ALLEY.

Sir John Hawkins dropped anchor in the harbour after capturing the Spanish *Madre de Dios* as far south as the Azores, and Frobisher set sail from Harwich to find the North-West Passage. Pepys was a member of Parliament for the borough and Nelson himself lodged at the 'Three Cups'. In this hostel I was privileged to sit, if not at the feet of the mighty (for they were well under the table) then at the same board. It happened this way. The great yachts had come round to open the season. We shall never see *Britannia* again, but she was there that day, with *Nyria* and *Lulworth*. One of the *Shamrocks* as well, all green and gold. The starting-gun fired but no boat sailed. Those huge new mainsails—and they *were* huge in those days—would have been hopelessly stretched out of shape and ruined on the first day of the season by that great cold wind blowing in from the east. The skippers therefore stepped ashore and by some chance I came to be at table with them. There was Sycamore, a barrel of a man, his little piercing eyes looking out from a mahogany-coloured face wrinkled like a walnut.

There sat Mountfield and Diaper, all great skippers, not only of that time, but of all time. They were men with great experience of such meetings. Big men who lined their stomachs well in order to contain, absorb, or support the enormous quantities of liquor they were later so easily able to consume. I can see them now, plates and dishes pushed aside. The east wind roared outside while historic races were re-sailed with the aid of matches and marks of fingers dipped in pint mugs. The awed listener heard 'straight from the shoulder and no nonsense' the candid opinion of such a notable figure as, for instance, the ex-Kaiser from one who knew him on that great 'leveller', the water. In that room talk at least was free and things were said which never went beyond the door. But, truth to tell, as the afternoon advanced reminiscences became a medley of sound and voices became blurred to one of that notable company who fell fast asleep. When the maid came in to make up the fire the young listener awoke to find his heroes gone, leaving behind a vast array of empty glasses,

156

ash-trays full to overflowing, a room stuffed with stale smoke, **and a** thick head.

In that house, though perhaps in a more austere atmosphere, Lord Nelson and his officers talked, as we did, of the sea. The admiral had come to Harwich in the *Medusa* with the idea in his head that the French might attempt a landing on the Suffolk coast. At the time when he wished to put to sea the wind came in south-east, making a beat of it, whereupon the pilots declined responsibility for the ship's safety.

As one may well imagine, this state of affairs was insupportable to Nelson, who got hold of a marine surveyor named Spence from Ipswich who steered the vessel safely past the Naze and so to deep water. The channel through which they manœuvred was named 'Medusa Channel' by Nelson's order, and so it is called to-day.

I should like to have been aboard when they carried out the move-ments. Even now with our smart, deep-keeled, knife-like vessels it takes a devil of a time to beat from the Guard to the Bell buoy against the tide. That piece of knowledge, however, is more than a hundred years old, and I expect Spence saw to it that the *Medusa* got her anchor **well before** low water.

CHAPTER IX

THE ORWELL

Of Philip de Broke, of 'Chesapeake' fame;
Of Candish who sailed round the world O.
Of Vernon who hatefully watered the rum.
(They nicknamed the felon 'Old Grog O')
But more than all these, I tell of a star
Which shines in the East like a jewel.
Sparkling enchantingly down to the sea
The wonder of Suffolk—The Orwell.

Anon.

WHENEVER I think of the Orwell I think of bugles. It seemed funny at the time. We had rushed down to Mersea from London one evening, tumbled aboard and put to sea in a hurry. Too much of a hurry. Because when we got outside and into the Wallet we found more than we wanted, and the projected week-end trip to the Continent had to be abandoned. After a dirty, uncomfortable night we ran in from the Sunk Lightship, coming to anchor under Shotley Spit at dawn.

I expect it was midday before we were awake, and being only the owner I had to tumble out of a warm bunk to put the kettle on for the crew.

Sounds of bugle practice could be heard coming from the naval barracks. For half an hour we put up with the din. At last one of my helpers could stand it no longer. Sitting up in his bunk sipping tea between puffs from the first pipe of the day he calmly said: 'If I had my way I'd take those bugles away from those cadets and hide them away somewhere.' A well considered and moderate statement; it seemed, as I say, funny at the time.

The anchorage in the Orwell, a few yards from the Shotley shore, is one of the best on the East Coast, being at once snug, handy for sea and full of interest. Soon after high water you will see columns of smoke advancing along the belt of trees up-river; soon coasting steamers swing round Collimer Point heading out to sea.

Later on, those dark green trees make a background for the beautiful shapes and colours of barges' topsails, which perhaps will anchor under Shotley too.

In the evenings great hootings as from gigantic beasts are heard; the Continental boats are getting ready for sea. When the day slides into the quietude of night a black form moves silently and with gathering speed upon the darkening waters, shutting out the lights on the Harwich shore one by one. Behind this piece of moving darkness and rushing headlong with it, a maze of brilliant pin-points follow, tiered one above the other. High overhead in solitary aloofness, keeping pace with the galaxy below, the two mast-head lights of the steamer cut the stars.

Below, the red port light, like the baleful eye of some monster seen by prehistorics, hurries on. The lights of Harwich flick into view again one by one as the vessel passes carrying with her a tall column of smoke. The stern wave, drawn up as the steamer gathers way, sets the bell on the Guard buoy ringing like a tocsin, making 'Shotley Spit' bow and curtsy. All sound and harmless fury, the waters break on the Spit itself, but the yacht at anchor feels hardly so much of its spite as to move the riding light hung upon her forestay.

The show is re-performed as ship after ship swings round the 'North-Shelf', bound for the Hook or across the North Sea to Denmark. There comes a time when the final wave expends itself frothily on the shore, when the querulous buoys relapse into quiet dignity to resume their everlasting vigil over the channel. How many pipes have been tapped against the rails of yachts as the little play comes to an end, and how many times has it been said as the stars come out: 'Well! It's getting a bit nippy out here—better turn in ready for the morning.'

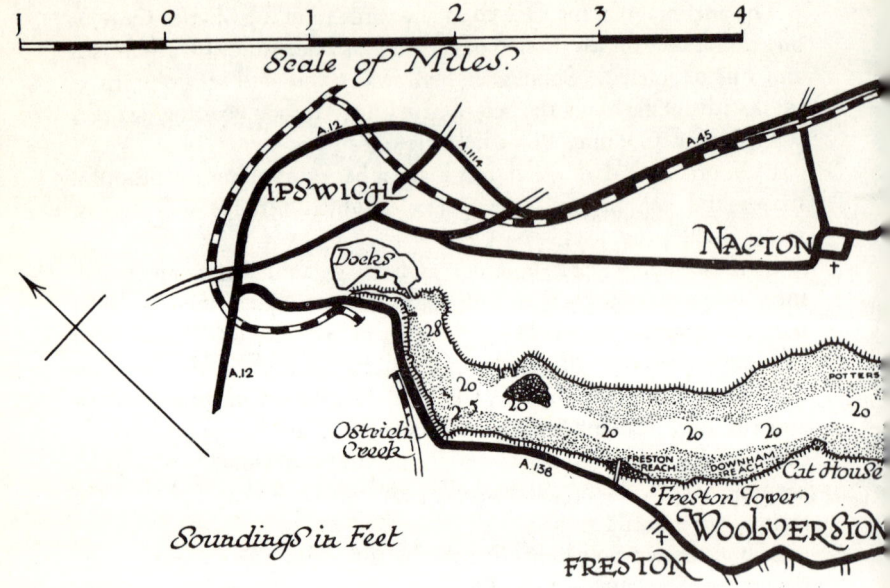

The Ipswich river has been likened to the Dart, but the well-wooded banks undulate, roll, or amble down to the water's edge rather than precipitate themselves as they do in the Devon river. At high water the Orwell presents a noble aspect; so wide does it seem, one fancies that all the ships of the world might sail upon it. But when the tide runs out to sea vast mud flats appear and all is enchantment. Great white clouds sailing aloft, reflected in mirror-like pools, skip from one to the other, touching them with the magic of colour. Rounding Collimer Point the panorama unfolds itself. Away up-river past Pin Mill, past the lovely parks of Woolverstone and Orwell, beyond Freston with its strange tower, in the far distance and veiled by a purple haze rise the mighty domes and towers of the great granaries at Ipswich, like a scene in the Orient.

160

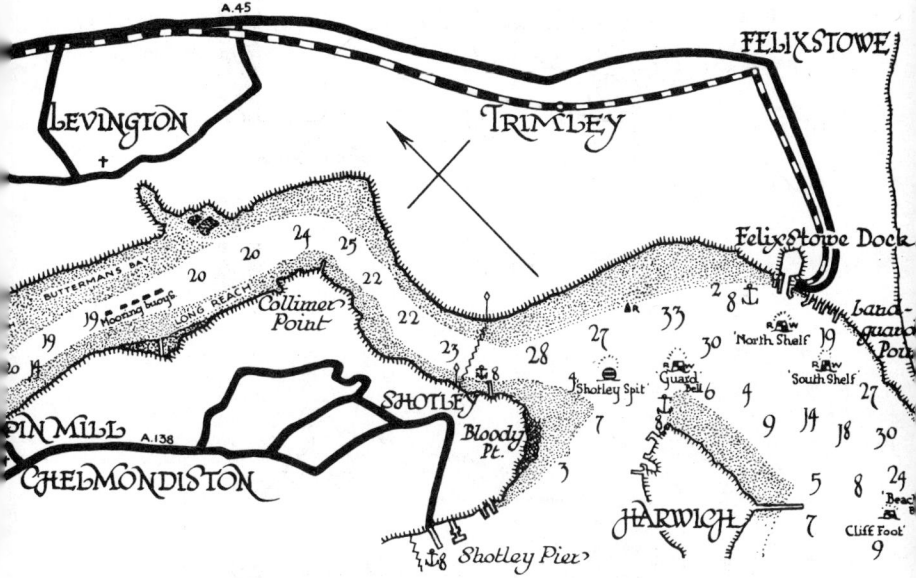

It has been said that at some time in their lives all Mohammedans go to Mecca; it might be said with equal truth that sooner or later all yachtsmen drop their hooks at Pin Mill. Having watched the building of my yacht there perhaps my judgment of the place cannot be relied upon. Through every stage of her building, from the laying of her keel to the never-to-be-forgotten day when she was launched (June 26th, 1937—a day full of sunshine, with a good tide, a good company of friends, a good ship and not too much wind to interfere with our purpose) all was pleasure. The smell of newly sawn wood, of paint and varnish, of tar and rope; the sight of *Concord*'s rounded (and noble) sides—the rustle of shavings as we walked round—the cunning-ness of it all is with me still.

Since I had determined to make the rigging for the vessel I became interested in 'serving' rope and therefore in serving mallets. A serving

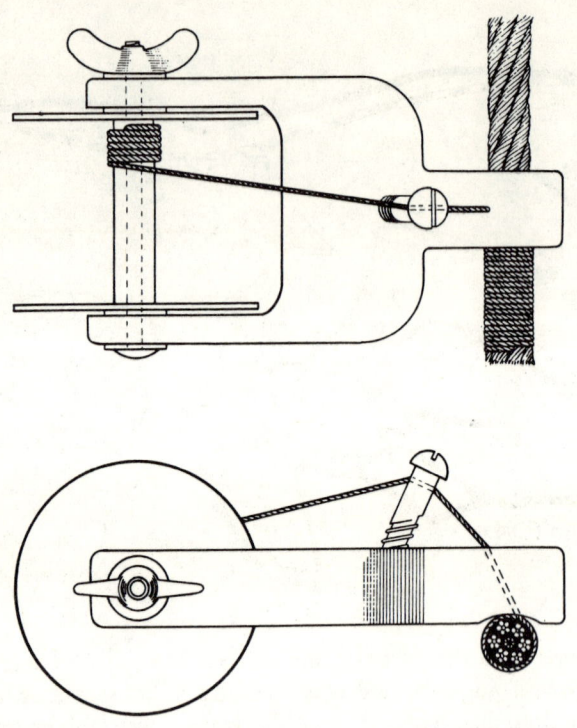

mallet should serve a rope quickly and efficiently. To do so it must carry its own supply round with it as it revolves. With all the 'professional' mallets I saw, one had either to pass a ball of twine round separately or the instruments were cumbersome and expensive. My grandfather's spade, which I had kept as a sort of trophy to his memory, had served him well; its blade, through use, resembled a trowel. Now its handle came to serve me as a serving mallet. Leaving five or six inches of shaft I cut off the handle and removed the iron pin and its wooden surround at the top. An empty reel on which wire for wireless had been coiled happened to fit the handle nicely, being held in place by a bolt carrying two washers aside, with a wing-nut for adjusting the tension. A hole bored at an angle comes out at the centre of a small curve cut in the underside of the shaft. Just above it, and also at an angle, a screw with a hole drilled in its top completes the tool. It is easy to disengage the reel in order to wind on a ball of twine the free end of which passes through the screw and hole in the shaft. To give it a start, the first turn or two is made by hand on the rope to be served. Thereafter, having adjusted the tension with the thumbscrews (there's 'spring' in the handle), the improvised mallet is spun round hand over hand in fine style, serving quickly and well. The diagram enables anyone to make the contrivance.

At week-ends during the building of *Concord* I used to sit at the bottom of a garden in what was once an

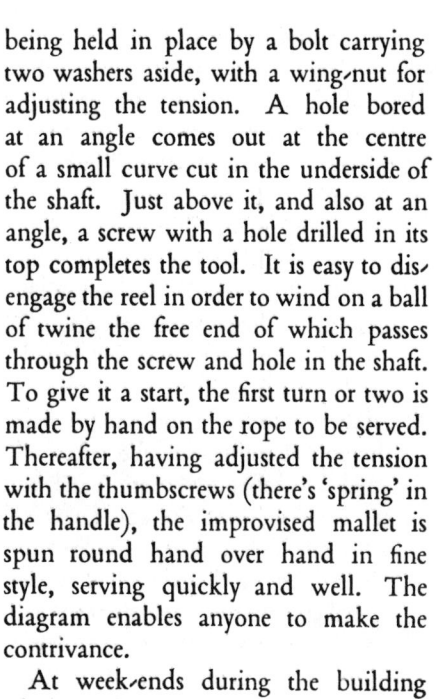

PIN MILL

omnibus watching the traffic going up and down river on the evening tide and listening as I smoked to Harry King, the builder, recalling his Spanish adventures when he and all the world was young and all Spaniards of those days 'full of fleas' and of no account. He used to speak of a man (whose indentity he concealed) who skimped on yacht **scantlings**—'and him a Methodist'. I used to watch a suit of

sails being made for me in surely the quaintest sail-loft that ever was. I have heard John Powell, the sail-maker, describe a loose piece of canvas as 'frubbly', an expression that enriches our language and says in a single word all there is to say. One is reminded of the cricket enthusiast who asked why a ball was called a 'yorker'. 'Well,' said the bowler, 'what else could you call it?' Powell's loft, next to the 'Butt and Oyster', once a chapel, was afterwards a bakery where vast quantities of bread were made for vessels sailing on Monday mornings to the West Rocks off Harwich to dredge stone. Two or three hundred boats were employed in the industry, not all, of course, from Pin Mill, but coming also from Felix-stowe, Harwich, Manningtree, and Mistley. The clay (Septaria) after being taken to a factory at Harwich went to all parts of the world, and it is interesting (or is it?) to know that part of the Calcutta Mint is made with clay from the West Rocks, which, it is said, sets as hard as stone, and weathers well.

The only road to Pin Mill leads straight into the Orwell; the long 'hard' thus formed is prettily lined with barges up for repairs, and yachts find the big stakes convenient to lean against for a scrub. The 'Butt and Oyster', under whose window one may row a dinghy at high water to drink a pint without the trouble of going ashore, was as well known to smugglers as it is to yachtsmen to-day. The road from the river inland is a pleasure to walk along; one looks down upon lovely old-world box-lined gardens with the beautifully proportioned square tower of Chelmondiston church dominating the valley.

Visiting yachtsmen seldom sail above Pin Mill, but the river is well buoyed and the two parks of Woolverstone and Orwell between which it flows are perhaps the finest in Suffolk—and the county is famous for its parklands.

Nestled on the verge of the river at Woolverstone is the 'Cat House', an old haunt of smuggling days where, in the night, a cat used to be placed in a lighted window overlooking the river to inform those 'in the know' that for the time being all was well ashore. Hereabouts that strange character, Thomas Colson, better known as 'Robinson Crusoe', sailed his crazy craft in search of fish. The *Suffolk Garland* describes him as 'tall and thin; his countenance meagre yet striking; and his eye sharp and piercing . . . his mind was so haunted with the dreams of charms and en-chantments, as to fancy that he was continually under the influence of these mischievous tormentors. His arms and legs, nay, almost

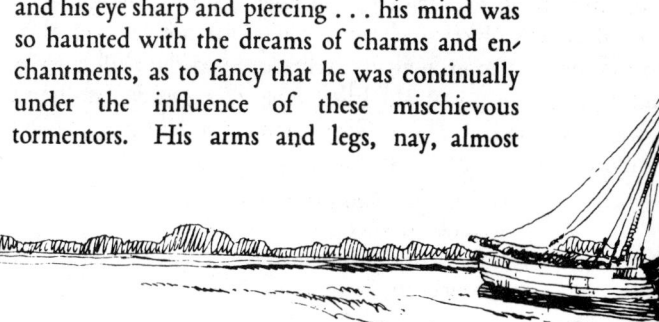

his whole body, was encircled with bones of horses, rings, amulets, and characts, verses, words, etc., etc., as spells and charms to protect him against their evil machinations. . . . When conversing with him he would describe to you that he saw them hovering about his person and endeavouring by all their arts to punish and torment him. His end came when a violent storm drove his ill-formed craft ashore; he was seen and earnestly importuned to quit his crazy vessel; but relying on the efficacy of his charms, he obstinately refused; and the ebb of the tide, drawing his bark off into deeper water, his charms and his spells failed him, and poor Robinson sank to rise no more.'

The poor creature played a not unimportant part in the strange tale of Margaret Catchpole whom we shall soon meet. In the trees a mile or so above the 'Cat House' stands Freston Tower, a queer edifice of six rooms, one above the other and each about ten by twelve feet. It seems to have been erected by a member of the Latymer family in the seventeenth century. Legend has it that the tower was built to let little Ellen de Freston pursue her studies unhindered, each room being set apart for a particular work. Imagine her then, between seven and eight in the morning, dispensing bounties to such as were abroad at so early an hour. The phrase 'as cold as charity' may be recalled, since the ground-floor room, though containing the only fireplace in the building, was, alas for the poor, without a chimney. Until ten, Ellen worked on a tapestry, ascending then for a couple of hours of music. From noon an hour was set aside for painting, a similar meagre allotment being devoted to literature. But her day was not yet over; there remained the topmost room with its arches open to the chill evening air. Thither the thirteen-year-old Ellen repaired to study astronomy (or did she?) Some lines 'by a Gentleman' in a *History of Ipswich* suggest a more romantic use for the top story.

> Here, perhaps, when winds were loud,
>   And the seaman's guiding star
> Hid her face behind a cloud—
>   Weeping o'er the drowning tar—

Sat some young and lovely dame,
  Feeding well the beacon flame,
Striving vainly to discover,
  Through the gloom her ocean-rover.

Above Woolverstone Park the river banks flatten out somewhat as Ipswich is approached, but a yacht can find five feet of water out of the way of the traffic at the mouth of Ostrich Creek, which dries out.

Ipswich takes its name from the Saxon 'Gipeswic', the river above the town still being known as the Gipping. It was always prosperous, and the Danes thought the inhabitants rich enough to pay a ransom of £10,000, a prodigious sum.

In the time of Edward III the burgesses found it worth while to pay two shillings 'a tun' extra duty on wine in return for added protection for her ships. By then the wool trade had become firmly established and not only the town but the entire eastern counties experienced a long wave of prosperity. And speaking of Edward III, the great

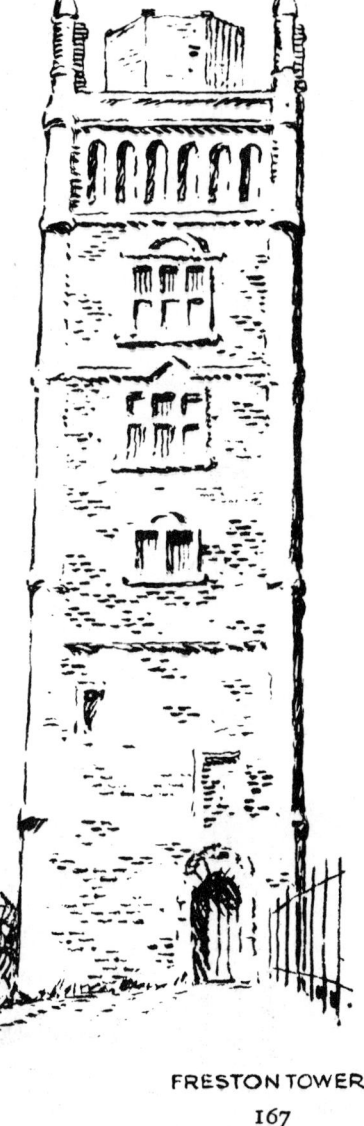

FRESTON TOWER

167

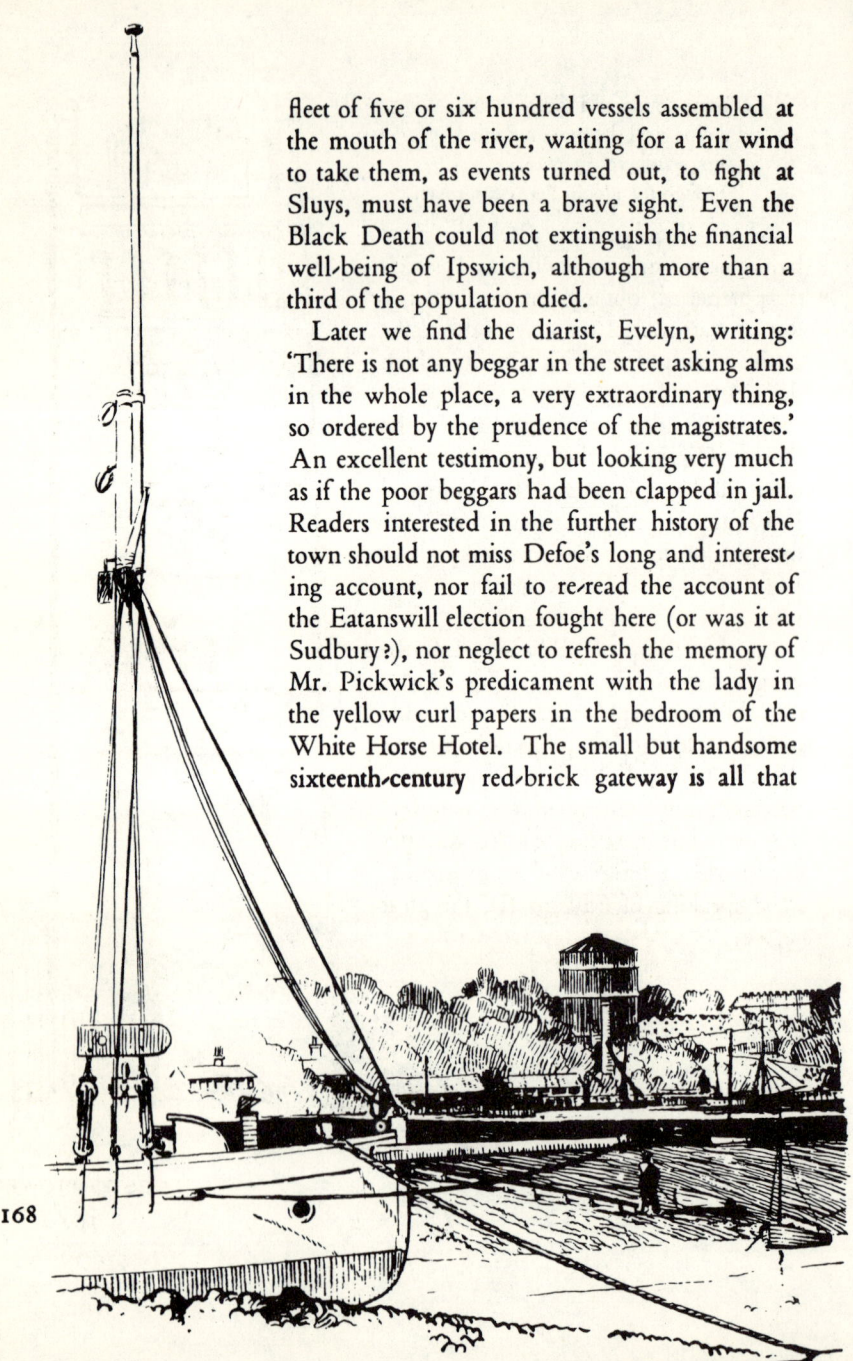

fleet of five or six hundred vessels assembled at
the mouth of the river, waiting for a fair wind
to take them, as events turned out, to fight at
Sluys, must have been a brave sight. Even the
Black Death could not extinguish the financial
well-being of Ipswich, although more than a
third of the population died.

Later we find the diarist, Evelyn, writing:
'There is not any beggar in the street asking alms
in the whole place, a very extraordinary thing,
so ordered by the prudence of the magistrates.'
An excellent testimony, but looking very much
as if the poor beggars had been clapped in jail.
Readers interested in the further history of the
town should not miss Defoe's long and interesting account, nor fail to re-read the account of
the Eatanswill election fought here (or was it at
Sudbury?), nor neglect to refresh the memory of
Mr. Pickwick's predicament with the lady in
the yellow curl papers in the bedroom of the
White Horse Hotel. The small but handsome
sixteenth-century red-brick gateway is all that

is left of Wolsey's grandiose scheme for the founding of a huge college, and it is curious that, after he had caused a magnificent tomb to be built for himself (it is in St. Paul's Cathedral, sheltering the mortal remains of Nelson), the grave of this most famous son of Ipswich should be unknown.

WOLSEY'S GATE

By far the most picturesque building in the town is Sparrowes House, or the 'Ancient House' as it is called. Cornucopia emptied her horn before the craftsmen who carved the massive oak pillars now black with age, for thereon are depicted riotously the fruits and flowers of the earth. The fine, lavishly carved windows set off well the plaster walls enriched by figures representing the four continents (Australia was then unknown) and by Atlas supporting the world. The flamboyant Arms of Charles II delight the eye, and there are garlands, birds, animals and scrollery of all kinds. Inside is a wealth of carved oak, a hammer-beam room, secret priests' rooms, much panelling and cunningly decorated ceilings, altogether pleasant to see, making the Ancient House one of the wonders of the eastern counties.

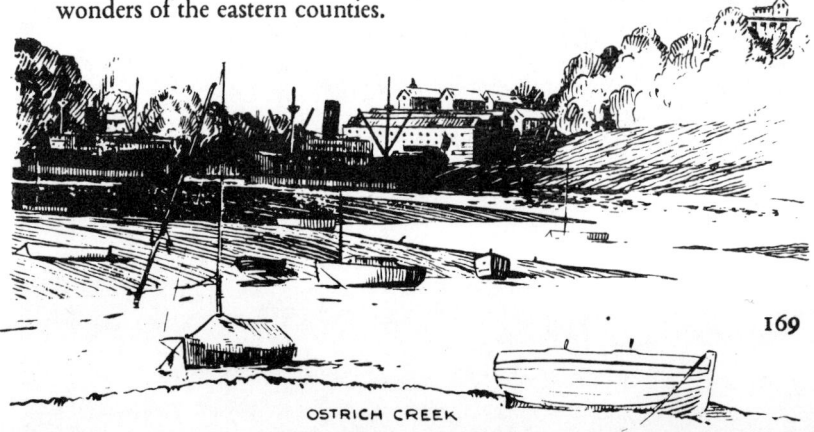

169

OSTRICH CREEK

Not so picturesque but nevertheless well worth a visit is the sixteenth-century Christchurch Mansion standing in the splendid park presented to the fortunate town by Felix Cobbold. Besides a large oak-panelled entrance hall with its mighty open fireplace it houses a great many interesting relics of Ipswich and Suffolk.

Leaving the town for Felixstowe we pass over Rushmere Heath, where Ulfketel fought the Danes and where, on the gallows at one time set up as a permanent warning to all, the man Kedgson was hanged. He confessed to having joined the army forty-nine times, thereby receiving as much as three hundred and ninety-seven guineas in bounty money. The pleasant lower road, with its glimpses of the river, takes us to Nacton and Orwell Park, the one-time residence of Admiral Vernon of Portobello fame.

In 1739 he spoke strongly in the House of Commons of the unjust treatment borne by Englishmen at the hands of Spaniards in the West Indies. Thereupon the powers that were dispatched the Admiral to put matters more to his liking, which he did by taking the town of Portobello by storm. The victory took England by storm as well, and

THE ANCIENT HOUSE.

upon his return Vernon received the·thanks of the Houses of Parliament and the cheers of an adoring public.

Towns all over the country were gaily illuminated, bonfires were lit, there were fêtes and jollifications of all kinds, and publichouses were, and still are, named after the gallant Admiral, thus showing the great tolerance of the 'trade', since it was Vernon who ordered every halfpint of naval rum to be drowned in a quart of water. The concoction came to be known as 'Grog' owing to the Admiral's habit of wearing a 'grogram' coat. A nice pun, my hearties--oh!--

> Smiling grog is the sailor's hope, his sheet anchor,
>   His cable, his compass, his log.
> That gives him a heart which life's cares cannot canker,
>   The sailor's sheet anchor is grog.

Nacton has another and equally famous admiral to its credit in the heroic figure of Sir Philip de Broke, victor in the historic fight between the *Chesapeake* and the *Shannon*.

Nor have we yet finished with admirals, for at Trimley, next door to Nacton, lived Thomas Cavendish, or Candish, the second Englishman to sail round the world. His adventures, recorded by Hakluyt, show him to have been a man of ferocity and determination. On one occasion three Spaniards were captured. 'Our Generall wrought so with them that they did confess, but hee was faine to cause them to be tormented with their hands in a winch, and to continue them at severall times with extreme paine. Also he made the old Flemming believe that hee would hang him; and the rope being about his necke he was pulled up a little from the hatches, and yet he would not confesse, chusing rather to die, than he would be purjured.'

Nor did his crew live a life of luxury. Consider their case in the straits of Magellan on the Admiral's last voyage during which they battled for five weeks in the dreaded straits without making progress. 'In the which time wee indured extreeme stormes, with perpetual snow, where many of our men died with cursed famine, and miserable cold—and all the sicke men in the Galeon were most uncharitably put a shore into the woods in the snowe, raine, and cold, where men of good health could skarcely indure it, where they ended their lives in the highest degree of misery, master Candish all this while being aboard the *Desire*.' Compelled by sickness, exhaustion, and adverse weather to abandon the plan of raiding the Spaniards at their Pacific back door, the fleet put back to the Atlantic where John Lane, ' a man of good observation', tells how in the night they lost touch with the 'Galeon' into which the Admiral had shifted. '...The whole fleete following the admirall, our ship comming under his lee shot ahead of him, and so framed saile fit to keepe companie. This night wee were severed, by what occasion wee protest wee know not, whither we lost them or they us.'

That was the last ever seen or heard of 'Worshipful Master Thomas Candish of Trimley in the Countie of Suffolk, Esquire'. The forty or fifty men in the *Desire* made their tortuous way to England after suffering incredible hardships. Off the coast of Brazil 'our dried Penguins began to corrupt, and there bred in them a most lothsome & ugly worme, of an inch long. This worme did so mightily increase, and devoure our victuals, that there was in reason no hope how we should avoide famine, but be devoured of these wicked creatures: there was nothing that they did not devour, only yron excepted: our clothes, boots, shooes, hats, shirts, stockings: and for the ship they did so eat the timbers as that we greatly feared they would undoe us, by gnawing through the ships side.' The wretched band struggled on, wasted by disease and hunger until 'it pleased God that we arrived at Bear-Haven in Ireland, and there ran the ship on shore; where the Irishmen helped us to take in our sailes, and to more our ship for flooting: which slender paines of theirs cost the captaine some ten pounds before he could have the ship in safetie—in this manner our small remnant by Gods only mercie were preserved, and restored to our countrey, to whom be all honour and glory world without end.'

During his three years' stay in England between his voyages Candish found the bones of a man on Felixstowe beach 'whereof the skull was able to contain five pecks, and one of his teeth is as big as a man's fist, and weigheth ten ounces.' Felixstowe is an ancient place, but no great deeds of valours were performed there, unless in private. Certainly the exhibition of the Dutch landing at Landguard Point in 1667 was devoid of bravery. Three thousand of them let fly with their small arms from the beach for an hour or so, whereupon a small vessel dropped a shot on the shingle, scattering the pebbles so frighteningly that the Netherlanders withdrew at once.

If Camden is to be believed, this 'Langer' Point at one time stretched two miles out to sea. There is a tradition that the River Orwell had its entrance north of Landguard Point, running south-east and across what we now call Walton Marshes. The land stretched as far as the West Rocks, where the ancient town of Orwell is said to have existed. The legend is very strong, and certainly there is no known reason for the river being called Orwell other than from the supposed town. Yet it is strange that there should be no exact information. We can go back to Roman times fairly confidently with no mention of it except hearsay. If it existed at all it must have been in British times. I wish I knew. These fascinating conjectures, like that about the lost Atlantis, always provide interesting if fruitless speculation, and I like to ruminate on the town of Orwell with its wattle-hut and woad-dyed Britons flourishing in the dim half-light of ages long ago.

CHAPTER X

THE DEBEN

I often wonder what the Vintners buy.
One half so precious as the goods they sell.

EDWARD FITZGERALD

THE lovely Deben is perhaps the least frequented of East Coast rivers; few motorists and not many yachtsmen know if its charm. The motorists are least to blame for this lamentable state of affairs, for extensive marshes extend from its banks and such roads as there are strike at the river at an angle, not running parallel within its sight, as is the case with the Orwell.

Nevertheless, the car takes one through fine and varied country, wide, windy, and gorse-covered heathlands making way for quiet, well-wooded country. On a fine August afternoon, if a great wagon-load of wheat comes ambling down one of those long, narrow, twisty lanes for which Suffolk is especially famous, take a look at it and the horses drawing it. Magnificent animals, clean-legged and powerful, bred specially for use on the heavy claylands—the renowned Suffolk Punch. Account it a piece of good fortune if you see a pair of them going to a horse show. Their always well-groomed coats have received an extra special polishing, and dangling to and fro the elaborate and brightly polished brasswork glitters in the sun as the noble animals, knowing that they are off upon some important event, stamp their newly shod hooves loudly and bravely upon the road. Neighing, they fling their shapely heads in the air, setting the brass ornaments all a-jingle. Their manes, cunningly fashioned to an intricate pattern with clean straw splays, open like a fan as they proudly arch their powerful necks. The tails have received the head horseman's expert attention also, being,

174

like the mane, entwined with new straw and bound with brightly coloured ribbon in the form of the 'bun' or 'top knot' so beloved by Victorian ladies.

A jovial old man, who was fond of pushing his drooping moustaches aside with the stem of his pipe, used to tell my cousin the tale of a parson, who, disliking 'top knots', preached a vehement sermon against the practice, using as a tag upon which to hang his denunciation the words 'top knot come down!' Giving Biblical authority for his astonishing tirade, he invited his startled and perplexed congregation's perusal of the twenty-fourth chapter of St. Matthew, verse eleven, where they read, 'let him which is on the house-top not come down'. The text might have served the Observer Corps during the war as a motto.

From Felixstowe to Felixstowe Ferry, or Bawdsey Haven as the entrance to the River Deben is also called, is but five miles by road. A queer, jolly little place, the settlement (one can hardly call it a village) seems to rest upon, rather than be an integral part of, the saltings. It is as though a gust of wind might blow it all away. The gay, brightly

A SUFFOLK LANE

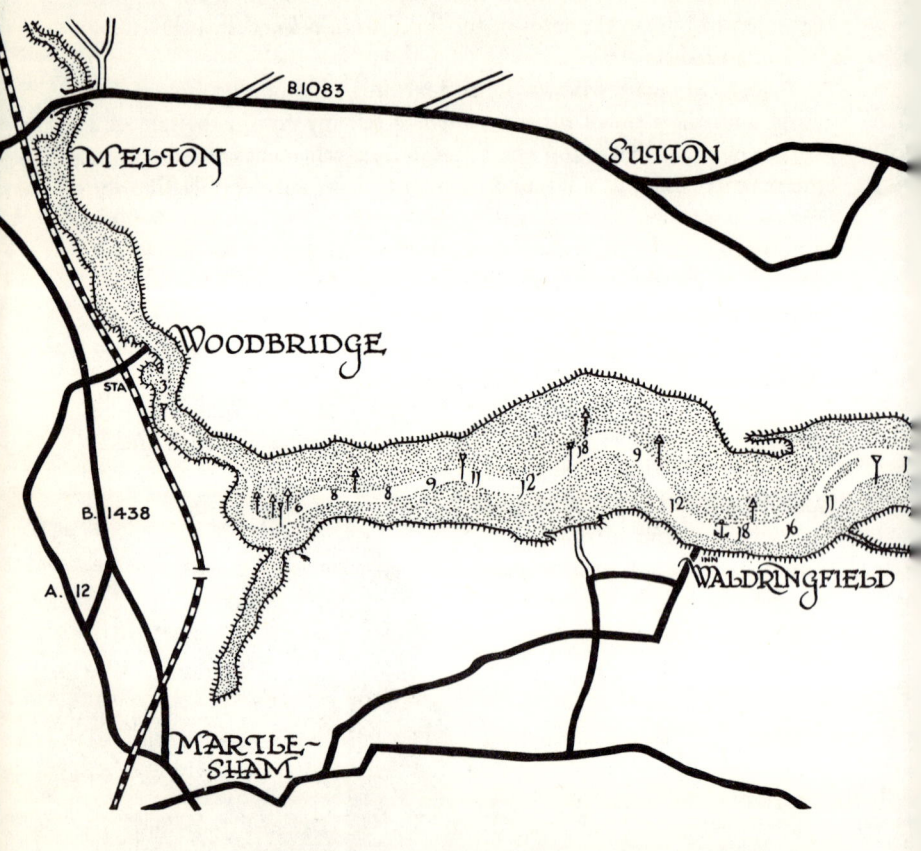

coloured roofs of the houses on the yellow shingle beach resemble those of more southern climes; from the flagstaff pennants seem to stream more bravely than elsewhere, and the larks' merry song mingles joyfully with the harsh cry of sea-gulls and marsh birds. It is an astonishing thing to see red earth in this flat clay country, and the bluff, pine-topped

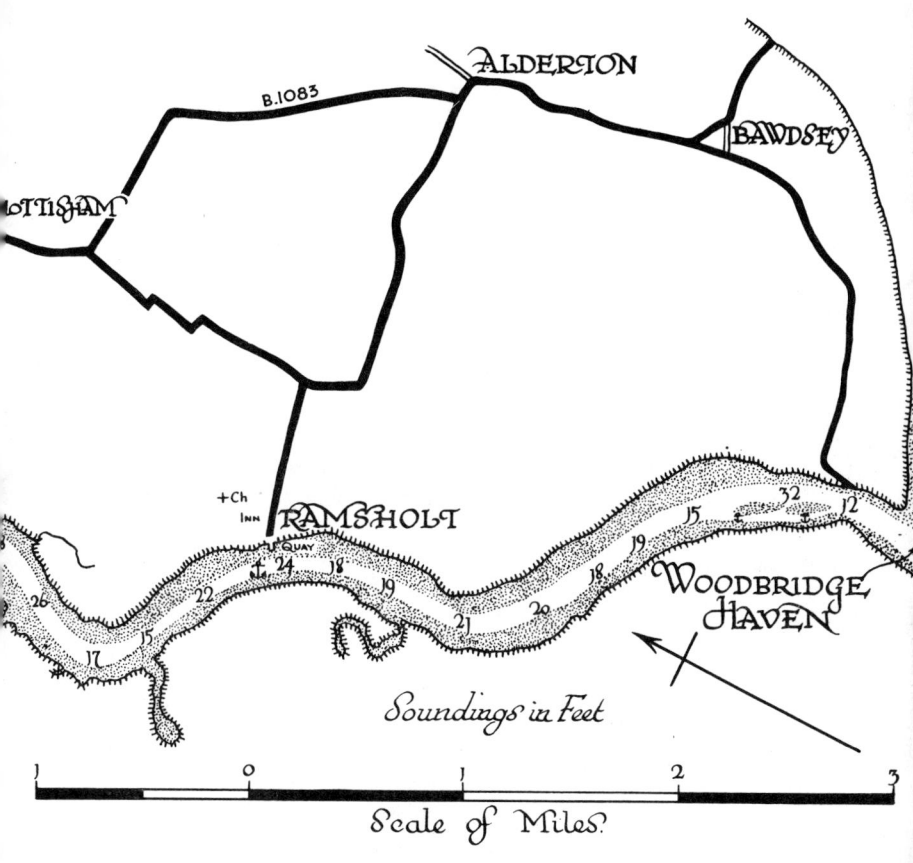

Soundings in Feet

Scale of Miles

cliffs of Bawdsey Manor give a theatrical appearance to the entrance
to the Deben. But the scene is substantial enough; the excellent inns
are no figment of the imagination, and certainly the two towers on the
beach are firmly implanted.

Martello towers take their name from Cap Mortella, a headland in Corsica. In 1794, during the French Revolution, a British fleet of five vessels arrived off the island to help local patriots. At Cap Mortella, defended by just such a fort as those now standing at Woodbridge Haven, they met with severe and prolonged opposition. The garrison of only thirty-three men, armed with but a couple of eighteen-pounders and a single six-pounder, and subjected to hours of heavy artillery bombardment, managed to stave off for hours the landing of 1,400 men before surrendering their burning fortress. Such a tough and prolonged resistance convinced the authorities of the particular formidability of the structures, and a great number were hastily built all along the 'invasion' coast from Shoreham to Aldeburgh, to take care of a 'D-day' which never dawned. Erected at the beginning of the last century, they mounted heavy guns, and served also as watch-towers and strong-points in the defence against the feared French invasion. They are all of the same circular, slightly conical shape and vary little in size. They contain vaulted rooms for the garrison, and the flat top is surmounted by a thick parapet concealing guns. Some twenty feet above ground-level and reached by a ladder, a door gives access to the towers, which are sometimes further defended by a circular ramparted ditch. The fortifications were in fact a return to the castle of feudal times.

It has been said that the entrance to the Deben should not be attempted in an onshore gale nor without the aid of a pilot. No yachtsman has any business to be just outside the river in an onshore gale, but should he be so unfortunately placed, one can only hope that he will be able to claw off into deeper water. In a predicament in which he would be more likely to need the help of a lifeboat it would be as idle to think of obtaining the services of a pilot as it would be folly for the pilot to attempt to give it. In fine weather, however, provided one's position is known and the tide serves, entrance to the Deben may be attempted confidently without professional aid.

About half a mile south of Bawdsey Manor, which is easily seen nestling in dark trees to the left of the conspicuous red cliffs, lies the

178

red conical North-eastern Haven buoy. From there in an easterly direction a black conical buoy marks the fairway. The best time to go in is about two hours after low water, or a little later according to draught. Just at that state of the tide, shingle hummocks and banks are still uncovered or their extent plainly marked by ripples along their steep-to edges. On a north-west course from the Fairway buoy two beacons, displaying white boards, are planted on shore. If the bar shifts they are shifted as well, so that if they are kept in line a vessel will pass in best water to the river proper. During the war the bar has evidently changed; the leading marks are now seen opposite the Ferry Boat inn. As it flows, the tide now gathering strength hurries the craft along parallel with the steep-to Felixstowe shore, and so long as one avoids the groynes running out from the beach all will be well until the usual diamond-topped posts marking a telegraph cable running from shore to shore are abeam. Now lies danger in the shape of an extensive 'horse'. Look astern and keep the farthest Martello tower just open of the nearest; so you will clear the southern edge, and if you

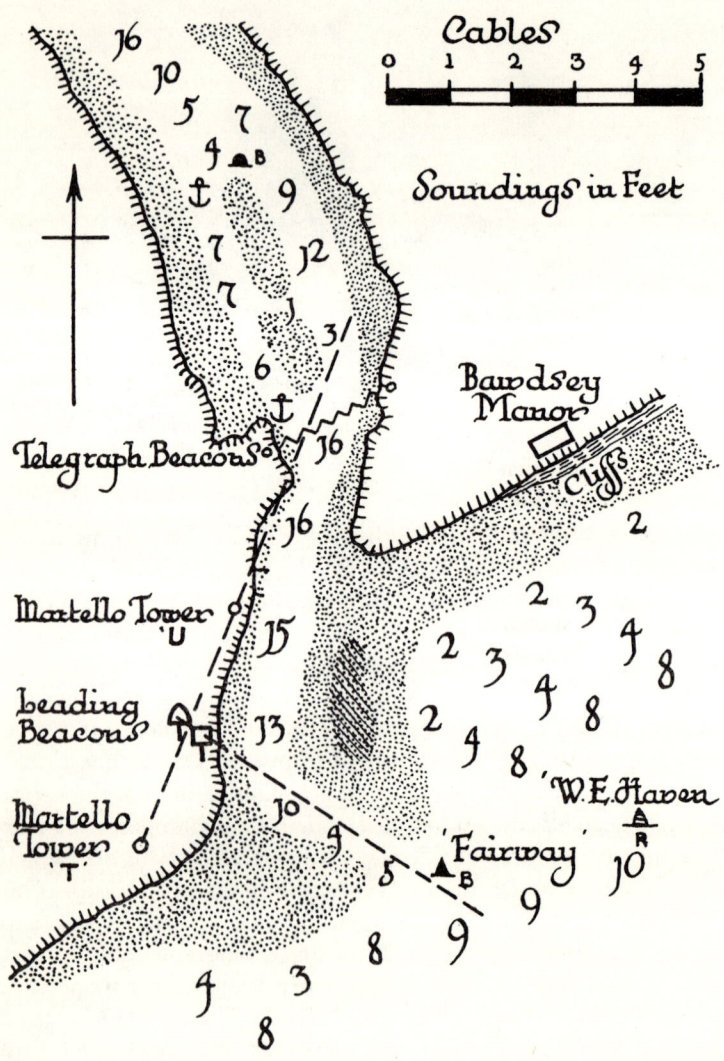

Cables

0 1 2 3 4 5

Soundings in Feet

16
10
5   7
4   B
9
7   12
7   )
3/
6
Telegraph Beacons   16
16
Bawdsey Manor
Cliffs
2
Martello Tower
'U'   15
2   3
2   3   4   8
Leading   13   2   3   4   8
Beacons   2   4   8
Martello   10   4   8   W.E.Haven
Tower   9   R
'T'   5   Fairway   10
B   9
8   9
4   3
8

leave a black conical buoy apparently in the centre of the river to port you will have avoided the entire obstruction.

There is a channel passing to the east of the shoal where yachts may anchor, but many moorings are laid athwart the stream. The only marks to show its width are ripples, and the lead should be kept handy. It is best to lie above the line of moorings at the head of the shoal where the channel joins the main river. There is a contra-eddy, and at the beginning of the flood one still rides to what appears to be an ebb tide.

Although yachts drawing as much as eleven feet can reach Wood-bridge, few vessels of that draught sail upon the Deben. There are no large yacht clubs to attract the wealthy, and 'white tops' and 'reefers' give place to tousled hair and bathing-slips on this delectable Suffolk river. Nor would I hold it against a man should he confess to having run aground upon its banks. Rather would I account it to his credit in admitting manfully the fate which overtakes us all. Stranding, however, brings about nothing more harmful than delay or health-giving and strengthening exercises at the end of a sweep.

The level marshes on either side carry the eye easily to the woods beyond, and one is able to sit at the tiller smoking a peaceful pipe after the turmoil and excitements of the entrance, admiring it all as one glides upon the placid waters, tide-borne to Ramsholt. Ramsholt is a very good place at which to bring up, with excellent holding ground, a good landing quay and foreshore, and a capital inn. It is indeed pleasant to sit on the little cliff in the heat of the day watching yachts drift idly below; to smoke a pipe, to make a sketch as I have done, or nod and 'drop off' for half an hour to the sound of a bumble bee busying himself about the yellow gorse. At places such as this the mind becomes easy and contented; there is no danger—nothing to guard against. The car, out of the turmoil of the road, rests near the inn, the yacht floats below as upon a mirror to be admired at leisure from a new angle.

Places such as Ramsholt were well equipped for the trade of

RAMSHOLT

smuggling; even though there may not have been a quay, there was always a conveniently hard foreshore on which to land illicit cargoes with facility, and always a road along which horse-drawn wagons and farm carts went by the light of the moon. Their wheels muffled with sacks, they distributed contraband goods to safe places before the stars paled with the onset of the day.

There is a general impression that smuggling started with the French in Napoleon's day, but it goes back much farther than that. During the fourteenth century English sheep were famous for their wool which was eagerly bought in the Lowlands, manufactured there and resold to us, so giving a handsome profit to the Flemings. Edward III, to encourage its manufacture in England, prohibited its export; but, even though a man caught in the act of defeating the law might forfeit a limb, or even his life, smuggling at once began and flourished exceedingly, not only because of the daring, ingenuity, and determination of the smugglers themselves, but also because they had the backing of the great majority of local inhabitants who, as receivers, were as deeply involved as they, and innocent people dared not turn King's Evidence in spite of offers of large rewards. The government, however, avoided the error of a New England state where a smuggling offence was punishable by a fine of 'twenty dollars, half of which to go to the informant'. This fine proved no deterrent, and the penalty was altered to one of 'fifty lashes', which turned out worse, since the law forgot all about the clause 'half of which to go to the informant'.

There was never the glamour surrounding smugglers which envelops the deeds of the knights of King Arthur and the Round Table; the romantic aura still exuding from the picturesque royalists of Charles's times has never fallen upon the salt-encrusted heads and shoulders of the 'free traders' or 'owlers' as they were sometimes called. A tough crowd, used to wringing a hard living from the sea, smuggling to them was 'easy money'—not that they ever got it. An odd cask of brandy or rum, a quid of tobacco, a silver shilling or two in his pocket, or a silken scarf for his light o' love was enough for a smuggler to run the risk as well as the cargo.

> Sing Ho, sing Hey, there's no time like the present—
> Sing Ho, sing Hey, there's no time like to-day!

was his motto, and every trick, subterfuge, or device to thwart preventive men was put into practice. Their luggers were superbly handled, but apart from skill, deceitfulness was employed. Vessels had false bottoms filled with contraband. Hollow booms and sections of enormous timbers concealed tobacco, an innocent piece of rope likewise; a silk

183

handkerchief might be tucked into the hollow heel of a boot, and many ingenious means were resorted to in anchoring casks in known places, to be picked up later when the 'air had cleared' a bit, or rather when providence sent a fog or sea mist. But a large cargo was bulky and difficult to conceal, and it was usually a case of watching for an opportunity to get it ashore to the 'backers' for distribution as soon as possible. The procedure required a large body of men both on land and afloat with a careful organization also. The ideal method was to direct the preventive men elsewhere when a cargo was to be run, but fatal clashes sometimes occurred.

One cannot but admire the preventive men who carried out their duties so manfully. Their numbers, like their pay, were small, and bribery was rampant. They were hedged about by rules and regulations in their efforts against determined men who, when in the mood, stopped at nothing. They were hampered by unsympathetic inhabitants, whose 'betters' were the prime instigators of the mischief. Parsons and lawyers, the 'old squire', and even the magistrate himself were all in the swindle and they, rather than the smugglers themselves, were the boys who made the profits. But with increasing pay and the clarification of their complicated status the preventive service (the father of our present coastguards) attracted a very fine type of man, and eventually the 'trade' was stamped out.

There was a later curious offshoot of smuggling little known and worth a mention. Vessels from the Continent laden with wines, spirits, tobaccos, silks and other heavily taxed commodities sailed out to the fishing fleets round the English coast. Coming alongside a drifter in calm weather, or putting off in a pulling-boat, they very quickly disposed of their shoddy goods at enormous profits. The poor fishermen, divorced for weeks from the land and its delights, fell easy prey. Rapacious skippers and mates aided and abetted the despoliation by advancing the men's earnings from their own pockets and taking a substantial rake-off at the end of the voyage. Therefore, after weeks of

184

arduous toil, the trawlermen stepped ashore already heavily in debt, his only future a repetition of the past, his past a bitter memory doubly paid for. The trade was known as 'coopering' from the Dutch 'Kooper'—a trading vessel supplying grog illicitly. I knew a Dutch-man who as a youth sailed in one such ship. He described how in the North Sea, all along the English Channel and even as far as the Irish Sea, they plied their profitable trade, until, as he said mournfully: 'It was put a stop to, although we used to fly the flag of the Missions to Seamen.' Almost the only article smugglers had difficulty in dispos-ing of was the famous Suffolk cheeses, unless as moorings, paving-stones, millstones, or for the ballasting of ships. The Suffolk poet, Robert Blomfield, wrote of it:

> Mocks the weak efforts of the bending blade,
> Or, in the hog trough rests in perfect spite,
> Too big to swallow, and too hard to bite.

Above Ramsholt (did I mention the unusual oval church tower with rarely fashioned Roman work?) the river winds pleasantly along with at least three fathoms of water to the head of Shottisham Reach, above which another 'horse' divides the channel. Its 'run' is shown by a beacon on the edge of the mud on the western shore, and by another similarly placed on the eastern side. Its extent can be seen by the discoloration of the water, by a calm patch, or by ripples on its edge. It is itself unmarked, so, while it is best to leave the shoal to starboard, there is no disgrace in running aground upon it.

From now on the river is marked by posts surmounted by topmarks pointing downwards on the port hand, upwards to starboard. Placed on the edge of the mud near bends and other artful places, they serve as guides to the channel. The mudbanks are extensive, but at Wald-ringfield deep water runs close to a beach, upon which one can land at any time with the yacht anchored close in, in three fathoms. Here are quays, boat-building and fitting-out yards, an inn also with sur-rounding country as pleasant as one could wish to see. Here the motorist and yachtsman join in pleasure, especially during regatta week, the outstanding local annual event.

Given a fair day all enjoy themselves. During the morning the bolder yachtsmen envelop all kinds of craft in immense volumes of canvas, forcing the vessels through the water as fast as they are able within a few yards of the beach in the view of all. After an interval for lunch fun becomes more general. From the committee boat a pole, liberally daubed with a nice mixture of tallow, grease, and salt water, is thrust out at right angles, supporting at its outward end the Union Jack. A figure in slips appears, rubbing his hands. Gingerly he puts one foot over the bulwarks on to the pole. Then the other. Standing poised for a moment he bends at the knees, straightens up,

arches his back, crouches, pirouettes, and wobbles, toppling backward at last to fall, amid thunderous applause, with a mighty splash into the river below. The greasy pole brings out a variety of technique. Some cautiously advance inch by inch, swaying as they go; others crouch their way along like tigers. Some attempt to slide the length of the pole gracefully, while a few, making no pretence at finesse, march boldly forward or even run in a vain endeavour to clutch the Union Jack (and the leg of ham which its capture entails) before they, too, plunge into the river.

There is the diverting 'pull-devil, pull-baker' when parties of men, stripped to the waist, strive to board and upset each other's dinghies amid a terrific paper-bag bombardment of flour from the one boat and soot from the other. Single- and pair-oared craft are driven at incredible speeds through the water, and 'crabs' are caught by the old hands for the edification of the hilarious spectators. It is a pleasure to watch graceful young ladies dive from the quay and swim a hundred yards with the tide and be hauled aboard dinghies by waiting longshoremen specially deputed for the task by reason of their great age.

The scene is gay. From the trees flags of all kinds wave, and yachts are 'dressed' in honour of the occasion. Periodically during the after-noon music fills the air. The local band, making full use of brass and percussion instruments, regales the assembly with such well-tried works as 'Zampa' and 'Annie Laurie' until, nearing tea-time and with a final clearing of saliva from mouthpieces, they bring the proceedings to a

WALDRINGFIELD

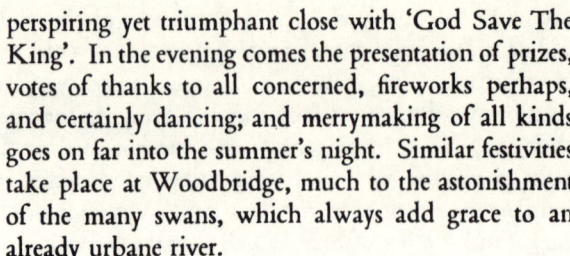

perspiring yet triumphant close with 'God Save The King'. In the evening comes the presentation of prizes, votes of thanks to all concerned, fireworks perhaps, and certainly dancing; and merrymaking of all kinds goes on far into the summer's night. Similar festivities take place at Woodbridge, much to the astonishment of the many swans, which always add grace to an already urbane river.

Celebrations of another kind took place across the river thirteen hundred years ago. In August 1939 the drums began to beat, a long way off perhaps, but nevertheless audible. There were rumours of men marching, of preparations for war. People began to wonder, but the papers found several columns of space necessary to describe and speculate upon the amazing discovery of a large Saxon burial ship at Sutton Hoo, on the eastern shores of the Deben. Only once before had such a thing been found in England, also in Suffolk, at Snape Common, but it was small, scanty in detail, and disappointing.

At Sutton Hoo the dozen or so tumuli were common knowledge. What they contained no one knew until their owner, Mrs. E. M. Pretty,

decided to find out. Three small mounds were investigated but, although interesting, their contents were not particularly so. A large tumulus was next examined, and it soon became clear that something of first-rate importance had been discovered. Experts from Ipswich, Cambridge, the British Museum, and the Office of Works were called to the scene. They found the exact mould of a vessel of about A.D. 600. The actual wood had rotted away, but nevertheless the precise shape showed clearly the form of the ship and its construction, even to indentations made by nails and other details. It measured eighty-four feet overall and had a beam of fourteen feet. Amidships a wooden structure containing a store of coins, weapons, and magnificent ornaments had been erected. The warrior's gold-mounted sword was there, together with a curiously worked whetstone to give it an edge. There were spoons and ladles, and magnificent gold buckles inlaid with garnet. So well preserved were the articles that the hinges of a purse, beautifully framed in gold, worked perfectly. Chief among the objects was a silver salver, three feet in diameter, its centre showing in relief the head of a lady.

It was at first supposed that the ship originally contained the body of Redwald, a king in Anglo-Saxon East Anglia who lived in A.D. 600. Afterwards authorities concluded that no body had ever rested in it (the king perhaps having been drowned and his body not discovered), and that the find was more in the nature of a cenotaph. The vessel had no mast but could accommodate thirty-eight oars, and had undoubtedly been used as a ship (having been damaged and

repaired), instead of having been specially built to contain a body as was sometimes done. Very likely she had been drawn upon rollers by horses and manpower from the River Deben to the 100-foot trench dug to contain her. The various possessions of the departed were placed in position and a huge mound of something like one hundred tons raised to serve as a monument for centuries to come.

At the 'inquest' held upon the 'remains' a queer point of law arose as to whether the discovery came under the heading of 'treasure trove'. Treasure trove consists of any gold or silver in coin, plate, or bullion found concealed in a house or in the earth or in a private place, the owner thereof being unknown, in which case the treasure belongs to the King. But, if it was abandoned and not hidden or concealed, then it belonged to the first finder, and the King's prerogative did not obtain. It is the hiding and not the abandonment of the object which entitles the King to it. Since the treasure found at Sutton Hoo was never concealed, except from the eye, but rather buried with the full knowledge and in the presence of a large number of people, the jury had no difficulty in coming to the conclusion that Mrs. Pretty was the rightful and sole owner. Whereupon, she generously presented the finds to the nation, and we are heavily in her debt when we are able to see the magnificent collection which is one of the chief glories of the British Museum.

'As red as Martlesham Lion' is a famous saying in Suffolk, and motorists who have driven down the main London–Ipswich road to Woodbridge, passing or rather stopping at 'Martlesham Lion' will know why. The inn sign makes a pillar-box look pink. With its gilded crown and scrollery, its claws, teeth, and eyes of gold, the monster scowls bravely across the road as it did, perhaps even more ferociously, from the prow of the Dutch warship it is said to have adorned at the battle of Sole Bay, in 1672. And as you tilt your glass in the parlour you will have the additional pleasure of seeing a splendidly carved oak ceiling.

Woodbridge, a mile or so on at the head of the river, is one of the most interesting little towns in Suffolk. In the market-place stands the quaint Shire Hall near by the unique 'weigh-bridge', which I have drawn for you overleaf; and all about the town are half-timbered houses, full of beautiful carvings, to describe which would fill a book. There are quays, together with boat-building yards, and John Fox would be able to find his way about his native town to-day quite easily, although more than three hundred years have passed since he walked those streets after his extra-ordinary adventures which Hakluyt so well describes.

Captured by the Turks in 1563 in a vessel called the *Three Half Moons* in the Straits of Gibraltar, he was carried to Alexandria, where, being a bit of a barber, he was able to obtain a measure of freedom, which he put to good use in plotting to make it complete. One dark night he liberated 266 other Christians, and together they marched down to the waterfront, possessing themselves of a galley. 'Whereunto every man leaped in all haste, hoyseing up the sayles lustily—now is this galley on flote, and out of the safetie of the roads: now have the two castles full power upon the galley,' says Hakluyt.

But in spite of a tremendous cannonade the vessel safely cleared the heads and, after a voyage lasting twenty-eight days, arrived at Gallipoli. Here they were rested, refreshed, and entertained by monks who 'kept there the sworde, wherewith John Fox had **killed the keeper,**

WOODBRIDGE

esteeming it a most precious jewell and hung it up for a monument'. From Gallipoli the party went to Taranto, sold the galley, and dispersed, after serving the King of Spain for twenty pence a day on the recommendation of the Pope.

Fox came home at last, where the court 'considering of the state of this man, in that hee had spend and lost a great part of his youth in thraldome and bondage, extended to him their liberalitie, to helpe to maintain him now in age, to their right honour, and to the incouragement of all true-hearted Christians'. Their 'liberalitie' and 'couragement' amounted to threepence a day, and I have often wondered whether that old sword of his still hangs in a monastery at Gallipoli. Relics thought much of at one time are apt to change their values, and I remember seeing a trinket containing the bones of saints—not of a single saint, mark you, but of more than one (though how many I

192

cannot tell)—sold by auction for the first, only, and ridiculous bid of half a crown.

A better-known though less martial native of Woodbridge, was Edward Fitzgerald, famous as the translator of a piece of Persian poetry which swept like a mighty wind through England and the United States. Societies and discussion groups were formed. The essence of the poem is 'eat, drink and be merry for to-morrow we die', strongly advocated by some, and as vehemently denounced from the pulpit by others. Illustrators, designers, and lettering men got to work on leather-bound, hand-tooled, and bejewelled volumes printed upon special paper.

The author, dressed in any clothes that came to hand, was

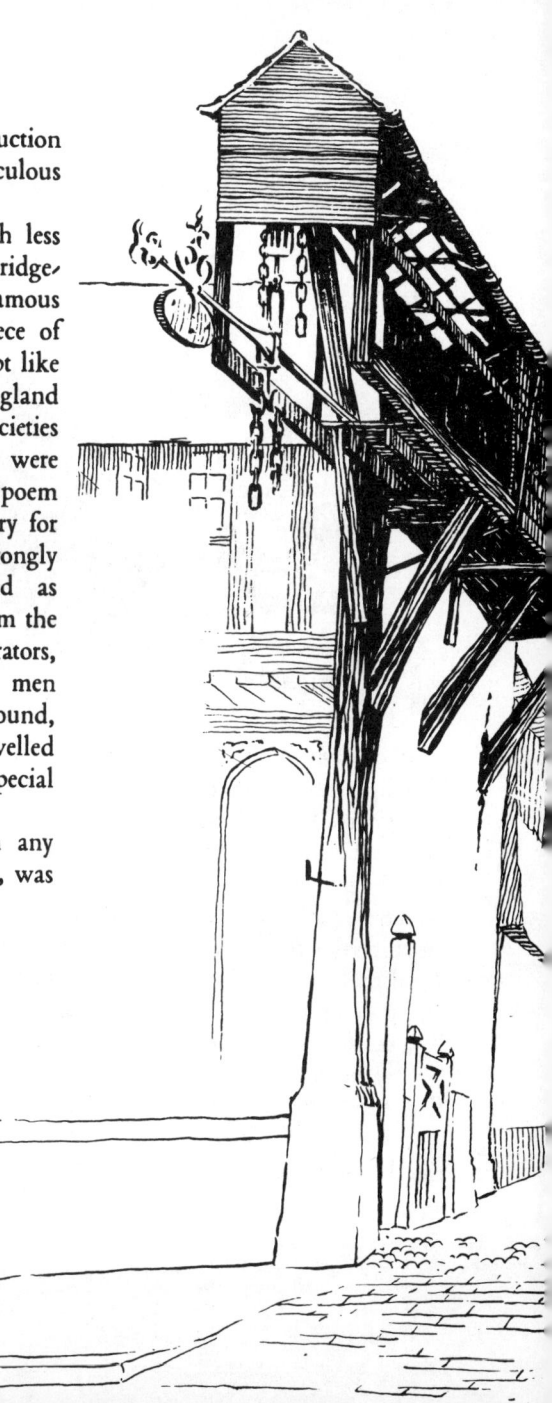

WOODBRIDGE MILL

greatly loved by the local children, who received coppers or sticky lollipops from his capacious and mysterious pockets. The famous illustrator Charles Keene would play the bagpipes to him, and such men as Carlyle, Crabbe, and Tennyson were his visitors and friends. Greatly interested in the sea, he had a schooner built at Wivenhoe which he called *Scandal* because, as he said, she travelled faster than anything on the river. Fitzgerald must have been a striking figure standing at the helm of his swift craft dressed in rough blue ill-fitting clothes, a tall dilapidated chimney-pot hat secured to his head by a scarf, and in cold weather his shoulders draped with a shawl. 'He came out like a soused herring,' said 'Posh', after Fitzgerald had been knocked overboard one pouring wet day at Lowestoft. But 'Fitz' stood his ground in the cockpit after his immersion, saying that he could not get wetter than he was.

194

'Posh', whose real name was Joseph Fletcher, was Fitzgerald's sailing master, friend, and co-partner in several vessels, but the two natures were fundamentally opposed. The author fell out with 'Posh' in more ways than one, and the association had to be dissolved with Fitzgerald patting the rough old seaman on the shoulder, saying: 'Keep from the drink, there's a good fellow.' Whether by taking the advice, or in spite of not doing so, 'Posh' outlived Fitzgerald by thirty-one years, and died in Lowestoft workhouse in 1915.

A seed was brought from the grave of the Persian tent-maker and singer of Naishapur by devotees, and from that seed a rose-tree blooms in Boulge churchyard not far from Woodbridge upon the grave of the translator of Omar Khayyám, Edward Fitzgerald.

> Ah Love! could thou and I with Fate conspire
> To grasp this sorry Scheme of Things entire,
> Would not we shatter it to bits—and then
> Remould it nearer to the Heart's Desire!

> Ah, Moon of my Delight who know'st no wane,
> The Moon of Heav'n is rising once again:
> How oft hereafter rising shall she look,
> Through this same Garden after me—in Vain!

CHAPTER XI

THE ALDE AND ORE

... nearer land you may the billows trace,
As if contending in their watery chase;
May watch the mightiest till the shoal they reach,
Then break and hurry to their utmost stretch;
Curled as they come, they strike with furious force,
And then re-flowing, take their grating course,
Raking the rounded flints, which ages past
Rolled by their rage, and shall to ages last.

CRABBE

OF all the rivers of England none has so many peculiarities as the Alde and Ore. Several change their name on joining another tributary, but none so far as I know changes its name half-way with no sort of break such as a lock, or bridge, as does the Alde and Ore. Above Orford the river is known as the Alde, below, it is called the Ore. While its entrance is composed entirely of shingle, yet its banks are mud with never a stone to remain unturned.

With the smallest rise and fall of any river within the estuary of the Thames) $7\frac{1}{2}$ feet at springs and $6\frac{1}{2}$ feet at neaps), yet it has by far the fastest-moving current, the stream sometimes debouching into the North Sea at seven knots on the ebb.

But the most peculiar thing of all about it is this. Ten miles from its mouth (and it runs fairly straight) it is still only a couple of hundred yards from the sea. No other river in England is quite like it, unless we consider the back of Chesil Bank, in Dorset—but there it is more of a backwater than a river. It is interesting to speculate on what happened years ago to form the long, low, narrow strip of land running to Shingle Street. A glance at the map shows the bank, never more than three or four hundred yards wide, running along the coast for

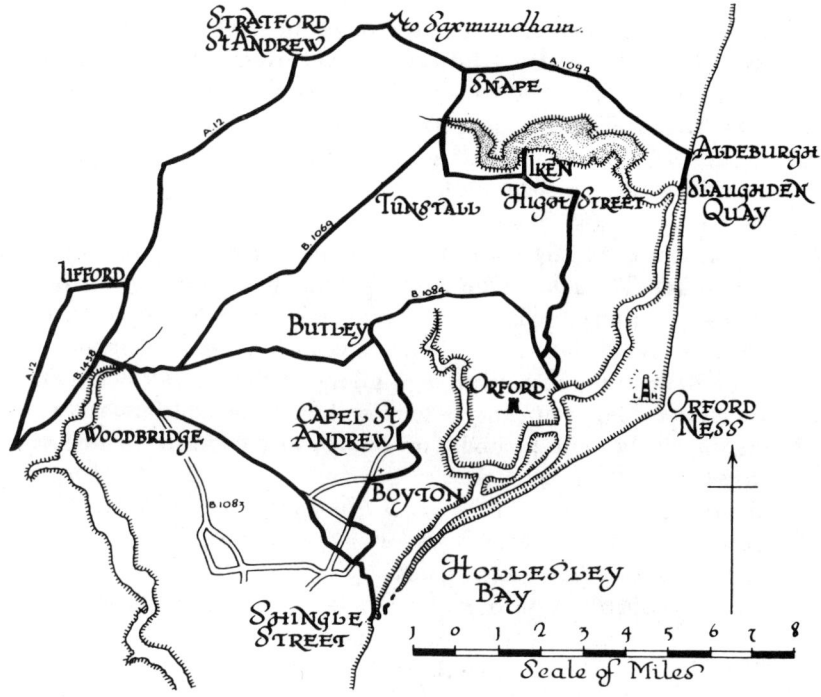

STRATFORD St ANDREW

to Saxmundham.

SNAPE

A 1094

IKEN

ALDEBURGH

SLAUGHDEN QUAY

TUNSTALL

High Street

A 12

B 1069

UFFORD

B 1084

BUTLEY

ORFORD

ORFORD NESS

A 12

B 1438

WOODBRIDGE

CAPEL St ANDREW

BOYTON

B 1083

SHINGLE STREET

HOLLESLEY BAY

1 0 1 2 3 4 5 6 7 8

Scale of Miles

ten miles. It seems only common sense that the Alde should enter the sea at Slaughden Quay. I dare say it did, once.

Standing only a foot or two above sea-level in the middle of the narrow neck of land at Slaughden Quay, the river on one hand, the sea on the other, a longing comes to be a boy again and dig a trench for the water to run straight into the sea as reason says it should, just for the fun of the thing; just to see what would happen. I expect the trench would silt up at the next tide and the river find an outlet farther south. For this reason. Ten miles north of Slaughden Quay there once stood the large and prosperous town of Dunwich. Once a very considerable port, it gradually dwindled in size and importance

197

as the seas encroached. It sent six vessels to swell the gallant fleet assembled at Harwich by Edward III; nevertheless, in that reign it lost 400 houses 'drowned by the sea'. The port altogether disappeared as the waters advanced, and now not a sign remains to mark the site of Dunwich; the ruins of the last of six great churches tumbled down the cliffs as lately as 1920, swallowed up, engulfed, and gone for ever. With the passing of the Dunwich headland the stream, sweeping close inshore where formerly a bay had been, began to move the coast bodily southward. The Alde, running straight into the sea, began to move as well, the shingle piling up gradually, inexorably forcing the river sideways. So the little town of Orford saw a waterway coming to it, saw it draw level and watched it pass, leaving it on the side of a river. As it crept along, grasses began to grow, solidifying and consolidating the shingle into firm ground, firm enough to support the lighthouse erected upon it. It crept onwards six miles beyond Orford before it allowed the river to enter the sea at Shingle Street. Or rather *below* Shingle Street, because it is within living memory that the Ore's mouth was two miles farther south.

Shingle Street! A queer, outlandish, savage place, inhospitable and bare. The motorist jogging along comfortably and pleasantly from Woodbridge will find his lovely Suffolk lanes giving place to flat, less wooded country; as he goes he will begin to notice deep ditches and waterways following the road on either side, until at length a great wall of shingle confronts him. Shingle Street! Through a dip the road leads to where the old 'Life Boat Inn' stood with a cluster of houses ranging on either side, flanked in turn by Martello towers. The charming little village had to be evacuated during the war, was used as a target, and blown to pieces.

When the river passed the inn, flowing out to sea below the Martello tower, old inhabitants will tell you how large brigs came in loaded with timber to discharge at the quay abreast the 'Life Boat'. It was a busy place then and prosperous. To-day no vessels lie securely guarded from the sea by a shingle bank; to-day nothing is left but large deep

SHINGLE STREET

ponds between the houses and the sea to show where the river once ran.

Sometimes a dinghy or two are pushed over the yielding shingle and set afloat to do a little fishing, but that is all. Only the stones are left, moved ceaselessly by the eternal swell which, falls it never so lazily upon the beach, yet draws a harsh grating note from the shingle it undermines and sucks to seaward on the ebb or heaps up on the flood.

That beach is never still, is never silent.

Two miles north, marked by coastguard houses on shore and a smother of white tormented foam at sea, lies the entrance to the Ore. Coarse binding grasses on the brow make for slightly easier walking than on the yielding shingle below. Here the beautiful pale yellow flowers and large pastel green leaves of the handsome sea-poppy flourish, three feet high. You may find also the creeping sea-pea. Its purple blossoms are rare in England, being seen only, so I am told,

199

along this little stretch of Suffolk coast. The two beacons ashore, moved as occasion demands, are the only marks to assist the mariner. To seaward there are no marks at all.

At high water with the current in a state of suspended animation it looks guileless. At the turn of the tide things begin to happen. After high water it is only a matter of minutes before the ebb attains a velocity great enough to prevent any but powerfully engined vessels from making headway. In all directions humps of shingle appear, growing larger, higher and more awe-inspiring as the tide-level falls, until at low water the entire entrance becomes an extensive mass, half water, half shingle. The mounds take upon themselves fantastic shapes. That seven-knot run of tide scours away their sides-forming beautiful easy, flowing curves. Some rise up fashioned like embattled towers perched on steep-to cliffs admirable for defence, others sprawl across the entrance resembling gigantic sea monsters half submerged and sleeping. Vast lakes containing small fish are fashioned. As the watcher sitting on the mainland surveys the scene before him, when all, as he thinks, is quiet at near low water, suddenly a castle, becoming top heavy, falls over with a roar and causes a few startled gulls to add to the momentary pandemonium. The last of the ebb slips out, still, however, running fast for an East Coast river, taking with it, perhaps, a treasured doll left on the tide-line by some careless child at Snape Bridge fifteen miles inland.

On a calm day to seaward, fountains of water shoot up as the swell falls lazily upon the outposts of the river. But with an onshore breeze of any strength the area around Orford Bar becomes a seething mass of tormented water. The incoming tide, rending and tearing at the defence in depth, pulls it down, undermines it, casts it aside, shifts it from place to another. All is chaos. The stream, forcing its way over an outer bank, takes upon itself the semblance of a waterfall as it rushes eagerly into a far-off lake, broadening and deepening it until it joins another and equally ferocious flow of water. One by one the outer ramparts crumble and fall as the tide, as if possessed of a devil, rushes on, submerging and swallowing everything in its path. Never-theless, the effect of the obstructions, battered though they are, remains, and is apparent still in the huge bubble-like humps of rising and falling water, and in the enormous swirls and eddies. On such days, when the tide has fallen again, what before was deep water may now be a knoll standing up with a side like the wall of a house. No doubt Orfordians know all about it (though I have seen them run ashore in calm weather), but for the visiting yachtsman who cannot know from day to day how things are on the bar, the best and only thing to do is to heave-to off the coastguard station at half flood and wait for a pilot to guide him over the four-foot bar to safety and delight.

After the rough and tumble of Shingle Street the yachtsman, now in calm water, has under him never less than ten, mostly twenty, and sometimes as much as thirty feet wafting him along to Orford. There are no navigational difficulties, the channel following fairly the almost steep-to banks with no extensive mud-flats on which to ground. Sail whichever side you like of Havergate Island, there is nothing to be gained either way. With the approach of night, anchor and rest peacefully in 'Abraham's Bosom' near Dove Point. Bring up here also, when preparing to leave the river; it is not advisable to anchor much nearer the entrance owing to the ferocity of the tide, which gathers strength rapidly as it ebbs and nears the sea. Here the Butley river joins the Ore, and small craft drawing no more than four feet can sail up to Butley quay at low water.

In the shepherd's cottage, formerly standing on Havergate Island, died the notorious John Luff.

' "There! There! There! I see him! He is not dead! No! No! No! There's Laud and Margaret Catchpole! Look! They laugh at me!" At last with one wild scream his spirit, like an affrighted bird, fled away.' He who brought nothing but trouble to everyone with whom he came into contact had ceased to live.

He appears in the Reverend Richard Cobbold's book *Margaret*

Catchpole. No work of fiction can ever hope to equal the true account of this Suffolk maiden's life. Margaret Catchpole in the service of the Cobbolds fell in love with Will Laud, an easily led character, who was greatly influenced by the wicked Tom Luff. For a time the pair were 'wanted' for smuggling offences, but Laud turned over a new leaf and joined the Navy. The service did him good, and his courage and resource with Lord Howe on the Glorious First of June obtained for him a free discharge, which enabled him to enjoy the

fairly large sum of money his uncle had left him. Soon, however, he drifted back to his bad old ways, and we find him again 'up to the neck' in the smuggling trade. Although she saw him only at very rare intervals during all these years, Margaret's feelings towards Laud remained unchanged. When she read what she thought was a letter from him imploring her to come instantly to London, she at once took one of her master's horses and rode the seventy miles from Ipswich in eight and a half hours.

In those days horse-stealing was a very serious offence, and a reward (details of which may still be read on an original bill in the 'Jolly Sailor' at Orford) was at once offered for the girl's apprehension. While trying to sell the animal at the Bull, Aldgate, Margaret was arrested; she was brought to Ipswich, tried, and sentenced to death. At the last moment the sentence was reduced to one of transportation to Australia for seven years. What with spending two years in Ipswich jail awaiting passage, and the remittance her good conduct would earn, it looked very much as though Miss Catchpole would be set free in her native town. But Will Laud now appeared on the scene. He had become implicated in the beating and throwing into the sea of the two coastguards of Southwold who had seen as many as forty farm carts standing ready for a 'run' at Dunwich. Hardly had this little affair blown over than 800 gallons of contraband gin were seized. So was Laud who possessed it. His goods and chattels taken, and saddled with a fine of one hundred pounds, Will found himself serving a year's imprisonment in Ipswich jail. Here he met once more the ever-faithful Margaret, who at the end of the year paid the fine, and Laud was once more free.

With all his faults Will was genuinely fond of his lover, and no sooner did he leave prison than he made arrangements for a vessel to carry him and his bride-to-be across to Holland. One dark night, and actively aided by Laud, Margaret absconded, and together the couple made for the coast. The sensational escape caused a hue and cry all over the eastern counties and a reward of fifty pounds was offered for Margaret's capture. See the couple now on Orford Beach. They are watching intently a pulling-boat approaching the shore from a vessel in the offing, her topsail aback, ready and waiting to bear them away from their troubles to happiness. Too late! They have not noticed the arrival on the beach of the jailer supported by revenue men. Margaret, turning round and seeing them, springs into the sea with a shriek. Laud, pulling her back, turns to confront the jailer, who demands his prisoner. Laud refuses. Then steps forward Barry, the
204

chief revenue officer, whose brother (mark this well, reader) has long been secretly in love with Margaret. A few angry words, a shot, and Laud lies dead upon the beach, Barry's bullet lodging in his heart.

Once again Margaret Catchpole was tried and found guilty, once again she was condemned to death. Again the death sentence was reduced to penal servitude, this time for life, and in 1801 she left England for ever, a convict, bound for Australia.

Having been twice sentenced to death and twice reprieved, having seen her lover shot dead at her side, having been sent to the other side of the world, one might be forgiven for thinking the story of her life had come to an end. In a manner of speaking it had only just begun! For in 1812 Mrs. Cobbold, with whom Margaret still corresponded, received a letter in which she announced her marriage with a gentle-man of considerable wealth and prominence in Australia. Who? Well, believe it or not, none other than the brother of Laud's killer—Barry, who had always loved her. What we hope (and believe) followed were twenty-nine years of happiness, and it was not until 1841 that the sorely tried Margaret was laid to rest at Sydney, honoured, respected, and loved by a large circle of friends and by many who had ample reason to venerate her memory.

The village of Orford was never very much larger than it is to-day, nor has much of historic importance occurred there. Certainly the Danes sacked the place, but in these eastern parts such an occurrence was almost a part of daily life. If Orford Castle surrendered to Louis, Dauphin of France, at the time of the conflict of opinion between John and his barons it did so without a fight, and although the little town sent no ships to contend with the Armada of Spain it helped on the financial side by contributing £39 9s. 6d., a fair sum for so small a place. Its corporation was dissolved as late as 1885 after a life of 600 years, and it was represented in Parliament until 1832.

From the fine quay a long street lined with picturesque cottages, inns, and noble trees slopes up gently to the church, the square, the Castle Inn (where they feed you well), and to Orford Castle. Built

ORFORD CASTLE

in 1165 at a cost of £1,407 9s. 2d. this favourite fortress of Henry II was in the nature of an experiment. The weakest parts of earlier square castles were their corners. To overcome the fault more corners were added until there were so many corners that there were no corners at all. So the round tower came into being, the strongest and most easily defended shape of all. Orford's twelve-sided keep was the work of Henry's official castle designer, Arnoth, who had a salary of sevenpence a day. Its walls, in parts twenty feet thick, housed a garrison of twenty men. These smaller fortifications built by the Normans all over the country acted as a sort of 'policeman'. So long as the castle was in the hands of the 'king's men' just so long the surrounding country remained 'loyal'. It was not necessary to maintain a large garrison in residence, for a small body adequately stocked with food (they generally had a well, too) could easily hold out for a long time until reinforcements arrived.

The little band of men at Orford had a bit of sport, according to the chronicler Ralph de Coggeshall. 'In the time of Henry II, when Bartholomew de Gladville was custodian of the castle, it happened that the fishermen, fishing in the sea, caught in their nets a wild man, whom in their wonder they brought to the castellan. He was naked and was like a man in all his members. He was covered with hair and had a long and shaggy beard. The knight kept him in custody many days and nights, lest he should return to the sea. He eagerly ate whatever was brought to him, whether raw or cooked, but the raw he pressed between his hands until all the juice was expelled. Whether he would, or could not, he would not talk, although oft-times hung up by his feet and harshly tortured. Brought into the church, he showed no signs of reverence or belief, either by genuflexion or bending of the head when he saw the sacred elements. He sought his bed at sunset, and always remained there until sunrise.' Once they brought him to the harbour and 'suffered him to go into the sea, strongly guarding him with three lines of nets; but he dived under the nets out into the deep sea, and came up again and again as if in derision of the spectators on the shore. After thus playing about for a long while, when they had almost given up hope of his return, he came back of his own free will. But later on, being negligently guarded, he secretly fled to the sea and was never afterwards seen.' 'Whether this was mortal man,' comments Ralph, 'or a fish simulating the human species, or some malignant spirit concealed in the body of a drowned man, such as one reads of in the *Life of St. Ouen*, is hard to say, all the more since wonderful tales of such events are told by many.' Very likely the poor creature was a seal. Through the generosity of Lord Woodbridge, who conveyed the castle to the town trustees of Orford, we are able to wander at leisure about the keep examining the many fine things therein and stand and admire the vast and wonderful view over land and sea from the battlements.

The church of St. Bartholomew, begun in the twelfth century, is nearby and worth a visit. Considering the spoliation it suffered in

1643 at the hands of the religious (and wicked) fanatic
Dowsing who 'brake down 28 superstitious pictures, and
took up 11 popish inscriptions in brass', the church is
fortunate in still being able to show a further eleven
brasses, one of which quaintly says of John Coggeshall:

> Pious he liv'd let that our pattern be,
> We shall be saintes; and so we trust is he.

In 1830 the top of the tower fell off, and remains
broken to-day; three bells were taken down and stand
near the font, the other two of the peal are still aloft.
The 'Farlingfield' of Henry Seton Merriman's *The Last
Hope* is easily identifiable as Orford, and there are many
local description in the book which make it, apart from
the romantic story of the Dauphin (or was he?), well
worth reading.

Above Orford the Alde runs in a general north-
easterly direction for five miles to Slaughden Quay, with
an average depth of seventeen feet. One might almost say
that so long as you do not run into the banks you

ORFORD
QUAY.

will never run ashore, so truly does the channel run. From **Slaughden** the river twists north-westward for six or seven miles to Snape Bridge, where it ceases to be navigable. Although the banks broaden out considerably, the channel so narrows and shallows that by the time Iken Quay is reached only half a fathom remains at low water with none at all at Snape Bridge.

At Slaughden Quay there is good anchorage with a clean landing at all states of the tide; petrol and water can be had and attention be given to a yacht in need of repair. For food we must walk the half-mile to Aldeburgh, a town which, though but a shadow of its former self, is still noted for its invigorating air. Here in Elizabeth's time was a largish port with a river and harbour. The *Marigold* was sent to aid in the destruction of the Armada of Spain, and four and twenty vessels at least, all above twenty tons, used the haven. Round about this time they built the lovely Moot Hall at the back of the town. Remaining unmoved, to-day it stands on the front! What we saw happen at Dunwich is being repeated at Aldeburgh, and the sea now roars within a few yards of the little gem of Tudor workmanship. Where houses, streets, and quays once stood is now deep water; the spray, flung high by cold winter onshore gales, flies unhindered against the leaded windows of the building; pebbles hurled from the beach assault and batter its walls. One day, unless the Moot Hall is moved (and it is worth the doing), it too will be engulfed by the ever-hungry sea.

On this bleak coast lived the poet George Crabbe—the first of the realists. After working as a shipwright at Slaughden and then as an apothecary in his native town Crabbe went to London with the idea of earning a living by writing. Perhaps he would have starved to death had he not taken Edmund Burke's advice and joined the Church. Back at Aldeburgh then, we find Crabbe installed as curate. In spite of his former ministrations as a doctor some of Crabbe's patients still lived. His short stay suggests they doubted his ability to cure their souls as they had questioned his competence to heal their bodies. But the poet-to-be, accepting the patronage of the Duke of Rutland at Belvoir, found his feet at last; his literary talents began to bear fruit, and his *Tales of the Hall* brought him in £3,000.

If George Crabbe is little read nowadays then so much the worse for those who can read. In *The Village* Crabbe is at his best, showing us the Suffolk scene, the fields and the woods, the birds of the air and the way of nature, tenderly and sympathetically seen. Nevertheless, of those with whom he had lived and worked he wrote pungently:

> A bold, artful, surly, savage race;
> Who, only skilled to take the finny tribe,
> The yearly dinner, or septennial bribe,
> Wait on the shore, and, as the waves run high,
> On the tossed vessel bend their eagle eye,
> Which to their coast directs its venturous way;
> Theirs, or the ocean's miserable prey.

THE MOOT HALL. ALDEBURGH.

Nor did he glory in his fellow man in describing the 'Oyster Dredger':

> He cold and wet, and driving with the tide,
> Beats his weak arms against his tarry side.
> Then drains the remnant of diluted gin,
> To aid the warmth that languishes within.

A dismal picture, my masters; yet Crabbe is not always so—he will conjure up visions of delight if you will read him. In the combination of vigour, gentleness, and charm he resembles the coast where he was born and on which he lived. Here in winter, when the cold north-easterly wind blows in from the sea, there is for ever heard the thunder of the ocean breaking upon the shingly beach; always the harsh, grating, pitiless sound, as a retiring foam-capped breaker snatches yet another inch from England's foreshore. As the year advances and the sun climbs high those same seas lose part of their strength and become more gentle. And if on a warm summer's day, with a nice sweet-scented sailing breeze coming off the land, that Old Man Sea filches a pebble or two slyly from the beach, perhaps when a new and sparkling tide is born, he will bring with him the little doll we saw going out on the back of the old stream at Shingle Street. Perhaps he will bear her safely through the turmoil of the entrance to the Ore and Alde, setting her gently to rest at the top of the tide on a warm sunlit bank at Snape Bridge at the feet of her little mistress.

INDEX

214